Virtual Survival

Staying Healthy on the Internet

Walter I. Zeichner

Crystal Point Publishing
Bolton, Vermont

Virtual Survival

Staying Healthy on the Internet

by Walter I. Zeichner

published by: Crystal Point Publishing
RR1 Box 5330
Jericho, Vermont 05465

Copyright © 1997 by Walter I. Zeichner
First Printing 1997
Printed in the United States of America

Library of Congress Catalog Card Number: 97-97131

Zeichner, Walter I.
Virtual Survival
Staying Healthy on the Internet
First Edition
ISBN 0-9661652-1-7

Cover art by Walter I. Zeichner
based on M100 Galaxy Courtesy of NASA

Contents

Feral Cyber
(mandala)

Acknowledgements

There are so many people to thank and appreciate. This list is in no particular order.

Jonathan Zeichner, Adam Zeichner, John Zeichner, Jesse Hendrich, Dana Davidson, Madelin Colbert, Amy Ludwin, Steve Peery, Lauren Berrizbeitia, Rita Zeichner, Abe Zeichner, Miriam Goldsmith, Maureen Joy, Elisabeth Forsberg, Elisabeth Hebert, Michael Lovetto, Aaron Goldberg, Linda Scott, Robbie Leppzer, Sara Morningstar, LilithEve Fletcher, Terry Lester, the Silverbergs, the Zeichners, Ann Peery, Trillium, Starhawk, Reclaiming, the self-selected affinity group and all the campers.

Thanks to the AOL Guides, you know who you are, but especially ILY, HMM, TIM, BR, CYA, EEK, EVB, KTQ, LDY, MOO, MC, MRS, NAC, MEE, ORI, VU, OUT, PET, REM, SLW, NAC, SUE, OOP, RGR.

Special thanks to Cyrus Moore for his help with proofreading and editing at the eleventh hour.

Very special thanks to the people who invested in this project: Gino and Michelle, Madelin, Jesse and Liz, Jace, Bob, Aaron, Loni, Terry, and Mary.

My deepest thanks to the cosmos we are all part of. It's an amazing entity!

Blessed Be!

About the author

Walter I. Zeichner lives in an intentional neighborhood in Vermont with his nephew John, 2 dogs, and 3 cats. An intentional neighborhood is a collection of people who have chosen to live in close proximity, each owning their home, in a mutually supportive non-communal group.

Walter practices psychotherapy in Burlington, Vermont. He received a Bachelor of Arts in Psychology and Education from Goddard College, and a Master of Arts in Counseling Psychology from Antioch University.

Walter paints, writes, meditates, practices yoga, gardens, and explores being a spiritual entity in the material world.

Preface

My first computer was an Apple IIc. I bought it in the mid 1980's. It utilized a ProDos operating system, had no RAM, no hard drive, and used 5.25 inch floppies. The monitor was monochrome. My next computer was an Apple Macintosh SE30; one of those all-in-one old style Macs with a 20 MB Hard Drive and 4 MB RAM. I progressed to a Mac Classic Plus from there, and then to an LCII, my first color screen! My next computer was a PowerMac, a Performa 6116CD which I still have. I then purchased a Powerbook 5300cs which I replaced with a Powerbook 1400cs/133CD. This book has been written, scanned, and typeset entirely on Apple Macintosh computers.

I first experienced an online service using my IIc. I don't remember whether it was CompuServe or Prodigy, but I didn't stay with it. The text based interface was not appealing to me. That was the mid 1980's. When I had my LCII, in 1995, I decided I wanted to be able to send faxes so I purchased a modem. The modem came with a free trial 10 hours on America Online, so I tried it. That changed my life!

I loved the graphical user interface. I loved the real-time chat, the ability to send and receive sound files and photos. I loved the content areas. I disliked all the technical glitches caused by both my computer and AOL, but I was hooked. I made friends online, I got involved with AOL's Community Leader program, and I started to learn about the Internet. I learned to surf the web, design web pages, utilize newsgroups. I loved the ability to do research without leaving home. I became someone who used (and uses) the Internet daily.

The Internet has grown and become a part of our global culture. The Internet presents a metaphor for global community; vast, diverse, essentially egalitarian, always changing, anarchic without being dominated by tyrants or terror mongers. There are hackers and thieves galore, and there are software and hardware manufacturers who seek to dominate the market, but the Internet itself is still what we, the users, make it. Anyone with access to the Internet can have a presence on the World Wide Web.

My work as a psychotherapist is based upon my belief in the basic health of the human organism, and our drive to regain that health when it is compromised. I believe that self-awareness work is deeply political, as well as spiritual and psychological. Personal liberation from inner and outer oppression empowers individuals to participate in the world as conduits for healing, for love and compassion. We are each capable of advocating for kindness, consideration, respect, for ourselves, each other and for the planet.

I believe that the Internet, still in its infancy, will have a profound influence on human culture. It already is. The more users who approach the medium with curiosity and an interest in self-awareness, the more the medium will have a positive influence on humanity.

Introduction

Our world is rapidly becoming a "Global Village." Politics, economics, communications; everything is changing. In spite of wars and ideological struggles our species continues to move toward unity. We have a long way to go.

Electronic communication is here to stay. Virtual Reality, cyberspace, the Internet, are part of everyday life for more and more people.

Spirituality has changed. "New Age" is no longer a fad, no longer news. People interpret and individualize spirituality to the point where they practice singular forms of worship. Organized religion is a significant force, but many acknowledge and act upon the need for a personal connection with God, Goddess, the divine, in whatever form they find it.

This book is for those who need to be connected with something greater. It's for people who are connecting through the electronic media; cyberfolk, onliners.

Millions are attracted to the abstract and imaginary, and spend hours sitting in front of computers and interacting in cyberspace. Nevertheless, the need for connection with the physical and spiritual is greater than ever. We use language and other mental tools for dealing with this new technology and its effects, and therefore we must reaffirm connection with our bodies, our emotions, and our spirituality as we extend our collective consciousness, disembodied, into cyberspace.

Cyber is in the mind. It's whatever we imagine. We connect through computers over fiber optic networks, but the connections really happen in our minds. We see the words, the digitized photos. We imagine the tone of voice, the sub-text and hidden meanings behind the words. We "create" the person with whom we are interacting, with varying degrees of accuracy.

Through inner/imaginal/awareness work we find connections with spirituality. My prescription for cyberfolk is to maintain awareness of the physical/emotional/ spiritual along with the mental (cyber being mostly mental). The alternative is to go dangerously out of balance, with ramifications of neglected health, extreme isolation, and quite possibly, due to neglect, the destruction of our environment.

Cyber is dangerous. People spend time online rather than relating "in person" with others. The very act of being "in" cyberspace is one of leaving body awareness and focusing on fantasy. Virtual Reality will soon provide complete fantasies; sexual, violent, mental worlds designed by programmers to fit a commercial paradigm. The realm of the imagination will be controlled by programmers and not by the user's imagination. The potential is a heretofore unimagined dulling of individuality and identity, all potentially leading to a kind of technototalitarianism, even brainwashing.

Millions of people have conversations online every day. They have cyber marriages, live in cyber communities, go to cyberschool, cyberwork, visit with friends, have sex, all in cyberspace. The medium of cyberspace offers amazing opportunities for connection and healing. (Those which we call "psychics" or "faith healers" are actually working with matter on the atomic and subatomic levels, as are people in cyberspace)

One night I was in a chat room on America Online. We were a community of about 30 people who met regularly in "The Refuge" to talk, play, flirt, and enjoy each other's company. "GonzoGirl," said she wasn't feeling well, she had a headache. I suggested that she take her hands off the keyboard, sit back, close her eyes, focus on breathing and relax. I began to send her energy, white clear light. I went into a meditative state and surrounded her with healing. In about 30 seconds or so she said

"Stop! You're making me dizzy!" I was a bit shocked at her response. I stopped. She reported that her headache was gone. I wondered how much of this was the power of suggestion so when we talked again a couple of weeks later without telling her, I started sending energy again, and once again "Walter, stop it! You're making me dizzy again!!"

By imagining, we create. What we imagine in our minds, we manifest into physical reality. Think of things you've accomplished and remember how they started. Creativity begins in your imagination. From there you take it out of your mind and into the world.

This book is about aspects of your life, starting with feelings, what they are and how you can put them into perspective so that they enhance your life. This book explores other facets of your existence as well, like your body, your creativity. Self-awareness is a step toward experiencing connection with the divine spark that IS life, made possible through the power of imagination; your ability to "see," "feel," and "hear" internally. Throughout this book you will be asked to connect with your body and your emotions, to develop your self-awareness.

Much of this material is simple. That is part of what makes it valuable. It is simple, easy to learn, and can help you improve how you experience your existence.

You'll encounter three voices in this book. One offers ideas and explanations. Another is personal, recounting some of my memories. The third guides you through awareness activities. Read the section called "How To Use This Book" for instructions that will help you to get the most out of the awareness activities.

I've spent 17 years as a psychotherapist and massage therapist. I've noticed that people tend to accept their feelings more when they feel "good." The painful feelings are often considered to be "bad" or "negative." What I believe is that feelings are just feelings. There are no "good" or "bad" ones. You can't control which ones you have but you can make conscious choices about how you deal with them; what you do and what you tell yourself. Becoming conscious of those choices leads you to accept the feelings you don't like, shifting your focus from labels, allowing you to feel feelings as they move through you so that you can make the most of your life. Let go of trying to bend the world to your wishes. You can't do it and you can hurt yourself trying.

Life isn't a neat set of boxes where everything makes sense. It's what is happening whether we like it or not. Accepting what you feel allows you to let go of the way you think things ought to be and to deal with the way things are. This is a form of telling yourself the truth. Rather than focusing on how you wish things were, you focus on how they are. Your power is in the present moment. This allows you to create your life more consciously, choose how you show your love and what your place is in the world. This will bring you to more conscious spirituality.

Are you addicted to being online? People can become so wrapped up in the online experience that they forget everything else, lose track of time and interests, and want to be online as much as possible. You can ruin your life on the Internet.

If you want to enjoy your time online and maintain thriving relationships with your health, friends, lover(s), family and community, then read this book.

How to use this book

Read these chapters with an open mind. Entertain new ideas, reexperience ideas which seem familiar. Give yourself the chance to see things from a point of view other than what you are accustomed to.

Your experiences are unique, but your humanity is something which you share. What I've learned can be of use to you, and what you learn can be of use to other people. Differences of age, race, gender, sexual orientation, economics and family status are on the surface. Go more deeply into yourself. Our species will come together in community as we learn about ourselves and connect with each other.

Do the awareness activities. Do them alone, with friends, partners, children, in small groups. Do them during breaks from online sessions. They are simple. You will have as deep an experience as you allow yourself. There are no right or wrong experiences. You will learn what is appropriate for you from each awareness activity.

The awareness activities are graduated, each preparing you for the next. They include questions. Answering them will help you gain more from the process. The questions are similar in each exercise, asking you to check in with your emotions, your body, your mind. This brings more awareness of your feelings, your body, your thoughts and your memories. The context of emotion, body, mind, and ultimately spirit, is the focus of this work.

I suggest using paper and felt tipped colored markers for the questions. Colors are fun to work with and they stimulate your brain. Don't limit yourself to the questions I have offered, but explore your responses to the activities any way you like, with movement, music, visual art, writing, and other expressions of your creativity.

1.
Danger!

You can lose yourself in cyberspace! Cyber is disembodied. What's at risk is your humanity, your soul, as with any potentially addictive behavior.

Cyberspace occurs in your imagination and it is limited by the confines of computer technology. Technology provides the "cyber" and your imagination is the "space."

Many people report that when they first start using a computer their dreams take on features of the computer interface. They dream in pull-down menus and keyboard commands. The sub-conscious has come in contact with the machine and is integrating it into the psyche. People spend days, weeks, and months obsessed with the computer. Some neglect their body, home, family, work, friends. Does this sound like any part of your experience?

Cyberspace provides an experience of being ungrounded. Since it happens on the computer and in your mind, it is easy to forget your body. People stay in cyberspace late into the night, forgoing sleep. Smokers smoke more. Drinkers drink more. Compulsive eaters eat more. The disembodied aspect of being in cyberspace heightens compulsions, in part because the need to experience the physical plane is heightened, but also because compulsive behavior is a form of avoidance. When one focuses on one's compulsion, then other critical issues are not dealt with. That is part of the function of any addiction.

We are more than just bodies. We have a bioelectrical relationship with the planet. When we lose touch with our bodies and the natural environment we become less well. Since computers are relatively new we have yet to see the long-term health effects of their usage.

Since cyberspace exists in your mind, in your imagination, everything you encounter online is interpreted through your thoughts, feelings, and ***emotional imprints***. An ***emotional imprint*** is a pattern of thinking and feeling.   These patterns develop during prenatal time, infancy, and childhood, though they can be formed anytime in life in response to one's environment. We do this interpreting with everything in life, but in cyberspace there is not always a reality check. All you have to go on is text, image and intuition. In a chat room the only information you have are words on the screen. There is no verification of the qualities of the person you are interacting with. In face to face interaction we communicate more with our tone of voice and body language than through words. Without those cues, in cyberspace, we count on text to convey more meaning than it is capable of.

For the cyber-addict, life revolves around the computer. Food is eaten in front of the computer. Cooking is about speed and ease of eating. Being in front of the computer is sedentary, so no exercise. Cyber is all on screen, so there is little or no talking with real people. No contact. No touch. The screen is hypnotic, just as television is. It is the kind of trance which can easily take you out of rather than into yourself. Without this knowledge it is easy to *not* develop new awareness, to just "trance out." Have you ever been online and lost all track of time or what is happening around you? Hypnotic trance can take you deep into awareness and into places of wisdom and learning. The online trance can easily be about leaving yourself, but it doesn't have to be.

You can make a conscious decision about what you do. Being online is similar to television because of the screen, which is a rapid strobe, and because of the electromagnetic properties. The major difference from television is its interactive quality. You can be part of the action in cyberspace, even if it's just text rolling by.

Spiritual growth requires going inside yourself for answers and wisdom while being conscious in the outer world. What we experience in the world outside ourselves is often a reflection of what's inside us. The more conscious we become of our inner world, the more effective we can be in the outer world. What we find in cyberspace offers as much in terms of learning about ourselves as what we experience in "real life." What you learn is determined by how you approach your experiences.

Cyberspace, as a social phenomenon, embodies the quintessential conflicts of contemporary society. We have an incredible technology which allows us to network with millions of people, but we do it by being alone. That is ironic. Humans need to be connected with one another. Technologized society is materialistic, competitive. Those qualities are not connections, they are about power in the material world which has little or nothing to do with spirituality. The kind of power which exists in competition is about individuals in a win/lose scenario, and not about the collective in a win/win scenario. Win/lose means that someone has to end up in the "one down" position. In a win/win no one has to lose. Everyone's well-being is a priority.

When people connect, their voices, touch, and gestures, are essential parts of their communication. When you connect in cyberspace you create a composite in your mind based on the information people give you (language, digital photo etc.), your intuition, your social experiences, and your projections which are based upon your own ***emotional imprints***.

There are millions of onliners who spend hours each day in front of their computers chatting. It's easy, immediate contact with little or no risk. One doesn't have to leave home or even get dressed.

We could become so obsessed with cyberspace that we neglect our society, stop creating the art and culture which nourishes, stop caring for the environment, stop having a dynamic political arena, stop trying to improve.

Relationships between friends have ended over cyberspace. Marriages have dissolved when one partner spent all their time with the computer and neglected their family. People have relationships online, fall in love, make plans, have cyber-sex. We can have dinner with friends, conversations, meet people, participate in discussion groups, see pictures of each other, attend parties. There are virtual communities online; groups of people who meet regularly as friends and colleagues, to discuss topics, flirt, share information and ideas.

We can meet people from all over the world, exchange ideas, find commonalities, support each other's growth, create communities, run businesses, all in cyberspace. Cyber is dangerous but it is not evil. It is a powerful tool which can be abused or can be wonderful.

There is an online language of text symbols which represent physical gestures - smiles, hugs, kisses, flipping the bird, being sexually aroused - on and on. They are called "Emoticons." Cyber communication can evoke emotional expression and emoticons are used to show emotion in the chat environment. :-) is a smile. ;-) is a wink. :-)*** are kisses. {{{{{}}}}} are hugs, =:-| is a face, so is }:-)>.

It's easy to give voice to one's hidden selves in cyberspace. Anonymity is inherent in the medium, so there is freedom to be anyone, to try anything, to act any way. Many people find that it's easier to talk with strangers online. There is little risk. You have control over the interaction. You can end it easily. You can present any persona. You can live in a fantasy. Fantasy can give respite from a difficult reality. That isn't wise in the long run however, because like any drug, once the high is gone you still have to deal with your life. An addict relinquishes all power to act and becomes a passive participant, surrendering to the drug.

Mature use of cyberspace is the key. How does one define mature use? We often consider the ability to moderate one's behavior as a sign of maturity. If you examine the themes of extremism and moderation in your own life, what do you see?

The benefits of cyberspace are many. Chief among them, the opportunity to meet people you wouldn't otherwise meet due to geographical limitations, and easy access to information. The opportunities for networking and research are unparalleled.

Since cyberspace exists in the realm of the imagination it is one's relationship with the imaginal that we are really talking about. How can you contact your inner magician who thrives on fantasy, nurture that part of you, and allow the magician to enrich your life without becoming a slave to the fantasy?

Those of you who sit at your computers know how sucked in you can get. You may have explored many of the aspects I have talked about so far. Ask yourself how addicted you are to being online. Did you ever imagine you would spend the amount of time you do in front of a computer typing to strangers? How much time do you spend online? How much time do you spend offline with people? How much time do you spend in nature? These are good things to be aware of.

There are very real things you can do so that you do *not* fall into cyber addiction. Cyberspace distorts perception of time. That makes it easy to forget about the rest of one's life. It's easy, then, to stay online more than you may intend. The way to stay healthy and to be a cybercitizen is to be sure to do things offline!

Humankind is at a crossroads. Mass communication makes it possible for our species to work together in ways which are unprecedented. The consciousness for this is being developed through the awareness work of individuals like you. We are accustomed to working toward our own satisfaction, yet many of us who have access to this technology are using it to create a greater sense of planetary community. The Internet makes the exchange of ideas easy.

Like all new technologies this one can go in many directions. The potential for harm is different than that of the atomic bomb. Cyberspace can't blow up billions of people. It can, however, serve to fragment our connections with each other. The possible negative ramifications of cyberspace are serious. It could contribute to the human species falling into complete social dysfunction, leaving us without the connections necessary for ongoing development. Cyberspace is dangerous because people can become so enamored of their illusions that they stop pursuing truth. That is the danger. Life must be about the ever deepening journey through the self into universal truth. That is the learning challenge we are faced with.

Cyber is dangerous but it is also wonderful. It has the potential to bring people together in unprecedented ways. I have become friends with people I otherwise would never have had access to. I have been party to powerful healing, through psychic means and interactions in cyberspace. These experiences have shown me the potential for the medium.

I believe that the essence of life can be found in healing. We can choose to live so that all or most of what we do is part of healing. The more aware we are of our choices and our actions, the more we are participants in healing the whole. When we approach our lives with the intention of healing, then we experience healing. When we act with awareness then our intentions are clear and the focused healing power of our actions is great. It cannot be stated strongly enough that our intentions matter. What we are focused on bringing into this world through our actions matters. What we believe about ourselves

and others makes a difference. How we build or dissipate
our energy affects the whole.

2.
Being

How do you experience your own life force when you are using a computer? Where is your attention? Is your self-awareness different when you are online from when you are not?

I close my eyes and focus on my breath. I am inside. I experience physical sensations. My body awareness increases. I feel my breath and I am aware of movement all over my body while air moves in and out of me. I feel blood being pumped throughout my body. I feel energy. I see energy. I visualize my body exchanging subatomic particles with my environment. I know this exchange is a constant part of the perpetual motion of the universe.

Here is your first awareness activity. Focus on increasing body awareness through your breath. You will use awareness of breath and body in the subsequent awareness activities. These activities can be part of balancing your computer usage with time focused on your body and emotions. Make a regular practice of doing awareness work away from your computer.

Awareness Through Breath

Sit with your back straight, supported by a pillow if you like. Close your eyes. Take a breath. Fill your lungs completely. Hold the breath for a moment, then take in a little more air. Feel the expansion of your chest. When you are ready, let the air out slowly, feeling your chest contract. Resume breathing.

Notice whether your breathing has changed. Notice the sensations of expansion and contraction in your rib cage. Feel your muscles stretching, your lungs inflating and releasing air. Allow yourself to feel movements throughout your body, the result of your breathing.

During the breathing exercise did you feel any emotions? Listed on the next page are some feelings/ emotions you may have experienced. Ask yourself about each emotion "Did/do I feel any?" Listen and watch for the answer. Feel it with your body and with your sense of the emotional. Accept the answers that come from inside you even if you don't fully understand them, or they seem irrational. Do that with all the questions after the awareness activities. I suggest that you take the time to write your answers using your colored markers.

Here are the basic emotions. Did you feel any of them?

Love   **Joy**   **Anger**   **Sadness**   **Fear**

Did you experience other feelings?

Did you notice physical sensation? Where in your body do you feel it? Were any of the physical sensations connected with specific emotions?

Did you notice mental images, thoughts or memories?

Were you critical of yourself at any point during the exercise?

Is there anything else you'd like to express about this experience?

You have completed the first awareness activity. There are no right or wrong ways to do these exercises, and no right or wrong results. Do them when you are away from or in front of the computer. Working with the questions will help you get more from each experience. Taking time to work with self-awareness allows you to learn from within about your own wellness.

***

The universe embodies two concepts I think of as "paradox" and "constant change." Paradox: everything must have a beginning and an ending, yet the universe, apparently, has neither.[1] Constant change: it is a fact that all of the universe is in a state of constant motion whether we detect it or not, and motion means change.

Every particle of my body has been a part of stars, planets, other people, animals, plants, rocks, oceans, and rivers. When my body dies and is returned to the earth (I intend to be buried in the dirt with no coffin), my flesh and bones will blend once again with the planet. Eventually this planet will become dust again, floating in space. My body, and yours, will continue on the journey of moving through the universe, part of everything.

According to physicists, the universe came into being by the event called the Big Bang. The material which precipitated the Big Bang had to have existed prior to the Big Bang. What was that stuff? Where did it come from?

Perhaps it had already been a universe and was changing, becoming this universe. Maybe that same transformation had already happened countless times before.

The universe is in transition. Physical matter, which accor-ding to the law of conservation of energy is constant yet in constant flux, keeps changing form but is neither created nor destroyed.

What is consciousness? I write these thoughts. You read and respond. The existence of consciousness indicates that there is something non-corporeal about our existence, spirit or soul.

> **spir•it** (spir-it) n. 1. a person's mind
> or feelings or animating principle as
> distinct from his body. 2. soul. 3.a
> disembodied soul, a ghost. 4. life and
> consciousness not associated with a
> body. 5.a person's nature.[2]

Spirit is not quantifiable. It is amorphous, not solid like stone or wood, yet there is form because I experience boundaries to my consciousness.

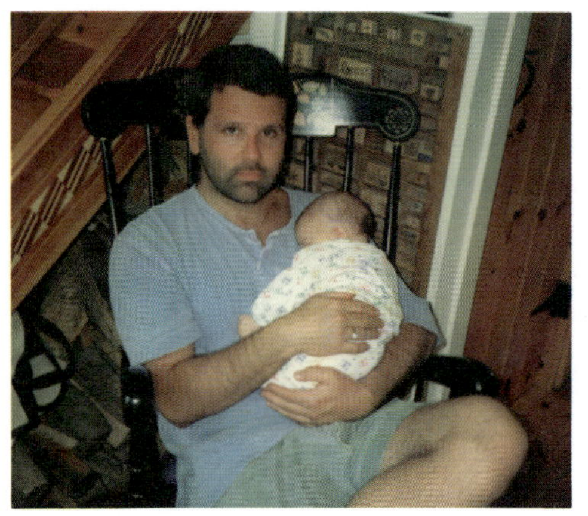

When I am with another life form I am aware of the differences between us. I and Thou. We are separate. Simultaneously I am aware of sameness; not just similarity but our oneness. We share life force which is and always has been undefined. We are connected at the foundation of existence. We are animated by some essence which is not quantifiable or definable yet is in all of us, every plant, animal, insect, microbe. The web of life is enormous. If you contemplate this then you will experience your connection with all life forms differently.

What does all this have to do with cyberspace? Besides the fact that the computer is a physical manifestation of the universe which you are manipulating and which affects you, cyberspace is in your internal universe. Whether you sit at a computer, meditate, or run, you are experiencing the reality you create. You create it by seeing the world through the lens of your beliefs, thus shaping how you experience the world. Your psyche internalizes your experiences in the world and makes sense of them so you can relate to the world.

3.
Physics & Psyches

The universe is energy. Energy takes various forms; molecules, atoms, subatomic particles. Particles vibrate constantly (except at absolute zero, -459.67°F, and below). They vibrate at different rates. They behave differently from each other. The vibratory rate of a particle is one of its characteristics. For example, color is defined as a difference in the wave length of light; red is a light wave of shorter length than purple. Look at the colors around you. Your eyes perceive different colors, registering various light waves differently. Physical matter reflects light at different wave lengths because of differences in particle vibration. Another example is that water at 55° Fahrenheit is liquid, while water at 32° F is solid. The particles are vibrating at different rates. Higher temperature indicates a faster rate than lower temperature. These are manifestations of the laws of nature which determine thebehavior of the physical universe.

Everything is made of particles, including you. Humans are small in relation to the whole universe, and so, in a way, we too are particles; microcosms in the macrocosm. Think of an onion, rings within rings within rings.

So it is with you. Inside you are cells, made up of molecules, made up of atoms, made up of subatomic particles.

When particles vibrate they create momentum which stimulates movement in the surrounding particles. Think of dominoes. Thought and emotion are the movement of particles in your brain and body, (a quantum event[3]) and these movements create momentum which in turn create more movement, more thoughts and feelings, each creating new movements of particles in the universe.

Thought happens in your mind. Thought is a manifestation of spirit, life force. It is happening in your brain which is a physical thing even though your mind is **not** an object or physical thing. Emotions and thoughts are actual physical events in the universe and all matter (particles) is a form of energy, so "Thought or Emotion = Energy in Motion."

Creativity comes from within as well as from the momentum of your life. Your creations are new combinations of thoughts and feelings, changes, and inspirations. We are creative beings.

Emotions are similar to thoughts in that they are also the movement of matter. Emotions differ from thoughts, though, since we feel them in our bodies. We need to experience our feelings in order to maintain healthy emotional balance. If we don't acknowledge and express our feelings, both physical and emotional health can be affected adversely.

Thoughts can result in emotions. Emotions can result in thoughts. You can invoke feelings by consciously or unconsciously focusing on thoughts which tap into ***emotional imprints***. When you are online interacting with people your ***emotional imprints*** are activated, as they are in other life situations. I believe that the amount and quality of information we get from a cyber experience is likely to activate ***emotional imprints*** because we rely upon imagination in cyberspace as we rely upon imagination when we project an ***emotional imprint***.

The purpose of the next awareness activity is to illustrate the following:

1. You can recreate emotions by focusing on specific thoughts.

2. When you "remember[4]" you are acknowledging something which is part of you, your memories.

3. You can honor your memories without allowing them to run your life.

Emotional Awareness
Invoking the Past

Remember an event from your life that was important to you. Notice what comes to mind as you comprehend the suggestion.

Remember as much detail as you can. Who was there? Where were you? When? What were the sights, sounds, smells, tastes, tactile sensations? Allow yourself to go into the memory as you breathe deeply.

Notice the experience of remembering. The list of basic emotions is below. As in the first awareness activity, ask yourself what you felt during the exercise. Notice your answers. Breathe and be aware of your body . Accept what you can of the experience even if you don't understand it all. Write about your responses with your colored markers.

Love　　　**Joy**　　　**Anger**　　　**Sadness**　　　**Fear**

Did you experience other feelings?

Did you notice any physical sensation? Where in your body did you feel it?

Were any of the physical sensations connected with specific emotions?

Did you notice specific mental images or memories? Here are ways to explore that.

Draw an image inspired by this memory. It can be a free form drawing of how you feel, or a picture from your memory. Make it what you need it to be. Focus on the process of drawing rather than on the product.

Make movements with your body that express how you feel about the experience you just remembered.

***

If you're going to spend time in cyberspace you need to know how to deal with feelings. Cyberspace is in your mind, it is also in your body. When you aren't aware of your body you are still a physical being and experience life through your physical form.

Your body remembers everything you experience. Your brain stores the memories chemically. You can invoke memories and the accompanying emotions, as you have just experienced. The sensations you felt in the last exercise were familiar. Your body remembers events through the sensations of sight, smell, sound, touch and taste just as your mind remembers the story of what happened. We store, for later reckoning, memories which contain unexpressed and unresolved feelings. The sensations from these memories manifest in our bodies as reminders or red flags saying "Deal with me!"

I've spent thousands of hours listening to people tell their stories with their words and their bodies, thousands of hours massaging people, touching them, reminding them to be aware. We need relief from pain, stress, touch-starvation. In relief we can find space to make changes. Sometimes memories surface during bodywork, and the person cries, rages, shakes with fear or laughter.

I've spent lots of time in cyberspace. I've felt emotions connected to things which happened online. My body feels and reacts. I learn from my interactions online as I do from offline. The relationships can have depth. One thing is for certain. I know I need to be in touch with my body.

4.
Fear

Fear is generated in your "old brain." Your old brain is the part of your nervous system you inherited from ancestors who existed before humans evolved into the kind of thinking creatures we are today. It contains basic programming for survival; instincts. It's in the part of your brain which occupies the back of your head and top of your spinal column. It's something we all have. This is where we get our "fight or flight" response. "Fight" to survive or "flight" if you know you can't win the fight.

People feel fear when they perceive danger or pain, physical or otherwise. People also feel fear when faced with the unknown. Fear can take over the fore of your attention, overshadowing thoughts, feelings, any other awareness. People also feel fear when they are disconnected from loving feelings towards themselves and others. Babies feel safe when they are loved, and that ***emotional imprint*** remains within most of us.

We are born with the ability to feel undifferentiated fear; hunger, cold, pain, discomfort. As we mature we learn the ability to differentiate between fear in the presence of real danger and fear where there is no danger. We need to learn that distinction or we spend our lives triggered into fear and not knowing what we're dealing with.

Fear is often experienced as physical sensations; tight muscles, excitement (adrenalin), increased perspiration, sweaty palms, increased heart rate, particularly hot or cold sweat, trembling, loss of physical control (sphincters), and other physical sensations. I'm sure you recognize these sensations from your own experiences.

Fear can stop you from enjoying life, being creative, loving, being loved, but only if you allow it. If you try to run from your fear it will catch you. If you try to deny your fear it will conquer you. If you are willing to go through your fear you will learn from it and enrich yourself.

Fear restimulates thought and emotion patterns from earlier in life; *emotional imprints*. These patterns differ from one person to another since we all have had different experiences. When we are very young the strong feelings we have, combined with the situations we are experiencing, are anchored in our memories. These memories help form how we see the world later in life. If feelings are not allowed to be fully felt and processed by the psyche, they generate particular patterns of behavior and belief systems based on that lack of completion. These beliefs are restimulated later in life. When we feel fear which is disproportionate to present events that is an *emotional imprint*.

Old fears and present fears differ. In present time there may be something to fear; a danger or unknown quantity which you need to be aware of and learn about. Old fears are like a lens, altering and distorting your view of the present. That's the activated *emotional imprint*. Fear is present but there is nothing actually dangerous occurring, or danger exists but not to the degree perceived. Noticing when this happens helps you learn to put fear into perspective. This frees up your ability to think clearly, allowing you to notice what is actually happening so you can respond appropriately. You may not be ready to respond to the present situation immediately, but at least you will know that the old responses and strategies (as per the *emotional imprint*) are probably not relevant. You'll also know that you can stop what you're doing until you are thinking clearly. With practice you will be able to respond more and more to what's happening in the present, not from your *emotional imprints* of the past.

There is also fear which arises because you are disconnected from love; not loving or feeling loved. That's the kind of fear which leads people to become mean, or stingy, to hurt themselves and others. That fear closes in on you when you feel worthless, and you don't believe in your own connection with the divine, leaving you bereft. It's a defensive fear because when you don't love or feel loved then you have to protect yourself from the hostile "outside world." When people feel victimized or have patterns of victimization this is often part of what's going on. When you feel stuck in a holding pattern, or uncreative, this is often what's going on. A simple way through this is to remember your actual connections with the universe, earth, people, your body, God/dess. Simple but not necessarily easy. Patterns of disconnection require deep awareness work so that healing and connection can happen. Patterns of disconnection are the result of early childhood situations where disconnecting was necessary for emotional and even physical survival.

Foreground/Background

Hold your hands in front of you, one a few inches from your nose, the other at arms length. Focus your vision on the hand in front. Shift your focus to the hand in back. Shift your focus back and forth a few times. Notice that you can choose where you focus your attention.

The hand you focus on is in the fore of your attention whether it's closer or further away. What you do not focus on remains, but you give it less energy since you are not attending to it. The same is true with thoughts and feelings. You can choose where to focus your attention and your energy.

Notice thoughts in your mind and pick one to focus on. Pick another thought and shift your focus to it. Go back and forth a few times between thoughts.

When experiencing an *emotional imprint* which distracts you from the present you can choose where to focus your attention. Pick an *emotional imprint* from your life. Notice the thought and feeling patterns. Notice how your awareness of the present moment is affected by the *emotional imprint*. Choose to shift back to the present.

This is an important skill to develop. You are regularly triggered into old patterns which can take energy away from your awareness and effectiveness in the present. By developing your ability to choose your focus you can make your life more satisfying.

In the next awareness activity you'll explore connections between emotions and physical sensations. We embody our emotions; experience feelings as physical. By increasing awareness of how you embody your feelings you are able to make choices about the role your *emotional imprints* play in your life.

Awareness of Fear

Acknowledge a fear you have. Focus on what you are afraid of. Focus on experiencing your fear. Feel the sensations produced in your body. Notice what happens with the muscles in your pelvis, belly, back, jaw, throughout your body. Notice how your breathing is affected. Notice any other physical changes.

Focus on one area where your musculature is affected by your fear. Breathe deeply, slowly, and intentionally. Allow the muscles in that area to begin loosening up. Notice your emotions and your thoughts. Do this with your entire body. What happened to the fear? Did it change at all? Notice what you can about the experience of fear.

Check in with your feelings. Ask yourself about each emotion and listen for the answer. Do your best to accept the responses from within you even if they don't seem to make sense. Use your colored markers to answer the questions.

Love   Joy   Anger   Sadness   Fear

Did you experience any other feelings?

Did you notice any physical sensations? Where in your body do you feel them?

Did you notice any scenarios from your past?

Who taught you about acceptable/unacceptable way(s) to deal with your fear? What did they teach you? Have those teachings served you?

Has being afraid ever created a barrier in your life? If you said no, how is it that your fear doesn't create barriers? How do you do that? If you said yes, how do you deal with the barrier?

Express your fear by vocalizing. Make a sound. Let something out.

You can change how you deal with scary thoughts. The next time you're scared, do some checking. Are you scaring yourself or are you in real danger? If there is no danger, how do you want to handle being afraid? If there is danger how do you want to deal with it? What happens to scary thoughts if you relax your body? Can this knowledge affect your life?

***

I think that many people are told to "get past your fear" or "just let your fear go." I believe that's unrealistic. Being willing to experience your fear, to go through it and to learn from it, empowers you.

Your first step is awareness of fear. Many people are distracted by the intensity of their fear and by the **emotional imprints** they carry, and they do not recognize their fear for what it is. They believe the thoughts "I can't" or "I am not good enough" or "This will last forever" or "I am trapped" or whatever they "hear" in their heads. Becoming aware that fear is "what's up" requires willingness to notice the mental chatter. When you notice that your thinking isn't clear you can take a personal inventory; physical, mental, emotional. Notice what is going on in the present moment and how it reminds you of something from the past. This is the act of identifying the trigger which is activating an *emotional imprint*.

Once you recognize your fear vis-a-vis the *emotional imprint*, you can separate old thoughts, beliefs, and feelings from the present. Pay attention to your body and your thoughts as well as your emotions. Check in with yourself a lot. If you're not sure how you're feeling, ask yourself and "listen" with your body and your mind. Accept the answers even if they don't immediately make sense. Old fears can ruin your life if you let them. Learn to recognize them, separate them from the present, and come to terms with them.

There are many ways to address fear. Once you have determined that you are not in danger you can focus your attention upon the physical, mental and emotional aspects of your fear. Your body is a powerful place to begin.

An effective technique is *"grounding."* This is the practice of extending energy and awareness through your body and into the earth using visualization and sensory awareness. This brings your awareness deeply into your for the moment. It is also an electrical event caused by the extension of molecules (remember, thought is a quantum event) through your body into the earth. There is always an electrical connection between your body and the planet. *Grounding* serves to make this connection more conscious, allowing you to feel the benefits consciously. The connection serves to balance out the flow of electrical current between you and the planet. This enhances feelings of wellness, brings you more into contact with the present, and out of the mental morass of fear.

Grounding can be done in many ways. You can create your own *grounding* technique. In the next few pages, either on your own or with a friend, read aloud while you do the activity. You can also record yourself on tape. Try it as written here first and then change the words in subsequent *grounding* to fit your needs. Do this indoors or out. I prefer to be out in nature but it is equally effective indoors.

If you get lightheaded during the *grounding* touch the earth or floor with your hands, relax and breathe, and you will feel better. This is good to do before and after using a computer since it gets you deeply in touch with your body.

Grounding

Stand with your feet shoulder width apart (take off your shoes and socks if you like). If you cannot stand, sitting or lying down is fine. Unlock your knees so they are slightly bent, not rigid. Allow them to be flexible, springy. Breathe deeply. Feel your breath expanding your lungs. Become more aware of your body. Continue to breathe fully as you begin to focus on an image; roots starting to grow out of the bottoms of your feet. Breathe and allow your roots to down into the earth. Let your roots grow deeper, through soil, layers of rock and underground rivers, deeper and deeper. Down through the bones of the ancestors and the dinosaurs, your roots are growing towards the core of the earth, the molten core still hot from the birth of the planet. Your roots reach the center. Feel the heat. Let your roots go into the liquid rock and allow yourself to release into the fire whatever

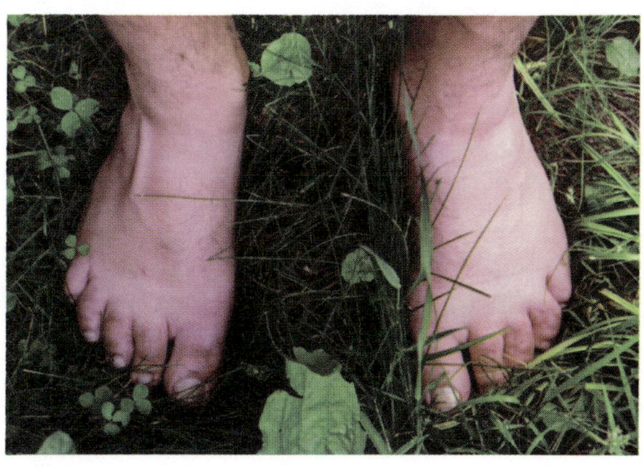

you are ready to let go of. Breathe. Let go of tension, old beliefs, anything you are ready to release. Let them travel down through your roots to the center of the earth where the fire can transform them. Fire burns and transforms. When you are ready, breathe and allow the core of the earth to feed you through your roots. Your body is made from the earth. The earth feeds you every day. Allow the earth to feed you in this way. Allow whatever you need to come up from the earth, through your roots, into your body. Breathe it in. Let it fill you. Breathe and feel connected with the earth.

When you are ready, begin to retract your roots. Bring them back through all the layers of earth, breathing, bringing your roots back into your feet. If you feel moved to, touch the earth. Look around. Remember where you are and what you are doing.

What was that like? What did you see? How did you feel? What happened to you? Check in with your emotions:

Love   Joy   Anger   Sadness   Fear

Did you notice changes in your feelings during grounding?

Draw an image. Allow yourself to express something about what you just experienced.

***

I strongly encourage you to **ground** yourself regularly while doing computer work. Try it and see what happens.

Another simple technique for **grounding** is to take a shower or bath. Water conducts electricity, so it serves to clear out your energy field.

As you learn to differentiate between **emotional imprints** and present time it will become easier to access your power in the present situation. I am not referring to the power of control or power over others. I'm referring to power in its immanent form[5]; personal power, aliveness, awareness, learning, the power of nature. This power is different from the power of hierarchy and domination and that difference is key in changing your relationship with fear.

Hierarchy supposes that power is limited and must be coveted, wielded by the strong over the weak. In nature, power is a complex web, interconnected with the molecular, atomic and subatomic, and everything in the food chain. When animals kill and eat one another they take what they need for themselves and their pack. They don't attempt to wipe out their prey.

You are part of nature. You can learn to share power; the power to speak your truths and the power to listen to others. The power you feel in a grounding exercise is different from the power you feel if you criticize someone. Try them both and see for yourself.

Meditation; I sit in the morning, upright on a pillow, my legs in a half lotus, my hands on my knees, thumb and 3rd finger touching. I close my eyes and listen to the silence. I hear the blood in my ears, the sounds outside my body, and something else. I hear a hum, a subtle vibration. It's the sound of the OM reverberating, the Big Bang, the ongoing vibration of creation. It is there, behind the silence. It is subtle. If I am thinking, I'll miss it. In order to hear it I must be witnessing my mind, in my breath, present in the sensation of each moment.

5.

Senses

Sight, sound, taste, touch, smell, intuition

When we are online often we are not fully aware of our senses. That contributes to the disembodied effect I referred to. It's a good idea to listen to music, have flowers nearby, or a view from your window which you can appreciate when online. Take breaks to eat good food, talk with someone, notice the sensations in your body. Ignoring the senses leads to over identification with the mind, and away from the physical, which isn't healthy. We are striving for balance.

Our senses are vehicles through which we experience the world around us. We ingest the world through our senses. If you eat or drink something, you are ingesting it. Food and drink go into your body and affect you. If you take nourishment you benefit. If you ingest a toxin you are sickened.

What about sounds, sights, smells, sensations on your skin, intuitions? You've heard sounds which produced an unpleasant feeling. You've seen and smelled things which disgusted you. You've been touched in ways which

which didn't feel good, or picked up "vibes" which left you feeling uncomfortable.

Do you watch movies or the evening news? When you see images of carnage does it affect you? How? What do the images and sounds of suffering and cruelty do to you? What about images and sounds which are loving?

Perhaps you've seen a beautiful view, tasted wonderful food, smelled a sweet or pungent flower, listened to music which moved you. You've felt love for another person, been touched with care. These sensations provide nourishment for your heart and soul.

Imagine what the world would be like if we consciously chose what to take into ourselves and what to put forth. Would life be different for our children? Would you make any changes in what you ingest and put forth?

I used to get the Sunday newspaper. I loved reading the comics and I felt that it was important for me to stay aware of what information the print media was putting out. One Sunday in July, 1995, that changed. There was an article on page 2 of my Sunday paper that horrified me, left me feeling ill for days. I felt like I had taken poison. I felt angry that this horror had come, uninvited, into my home. I canceled my subscription to the newspa-

per. I know that people do awful things to other people, but I do my best to determine when and how I am exposed to the more horrible aspects of life. Home is a sanctuary. I want it to be as safe as possible. I know that's not always possible, but I feel better, healthier, more able to respond to my community when I am feeling nourished by my life, not sickened over news coverage of abuse.

I have deliberately not described here what was in that newspaper article. This is an opportunity to make a choice about what you take into yourself. A brief description is in the back of the book[6].

Computer use offers the choice of what information you take in. There is also the random stumbling upon information that occurs when you surf the world wide web. The great thing is that you can choose what you click on.

Choosing what you take into yourself affects how you experience the world. That is true both online and off. If you do not experience some of the physical good of the world then your feelings will reflect that. Exploring your relationship with nature can only enrich you.

Being Aware of Beauty

Think about the adults who were important to you when you were a child. Do you think anything would have been different for you if they had experienced more beauty in their lives?

Each day for a week spend 5 minutes paying attention to an aspect of nature; a flower, the sky, a blade of grass, an animal, a child, a mountain, anything. Allow your senses to take in, to receive from nature. Be sure to breathe fully. What aspect of nature did you pay attention to today?

Remember the sights, sounds, tastes, smells, skin sensations you experienced. How did they feel?

Love   Joy   Anger   Sadness   Fear

Other feelings? Physical sensations? Where do you feel them in your body?

Is this something you do in your life?

Take the time to do this every day for a week and you will find that your awareness changes.

Keep a journal for the week. Be aware of your emotions, your body, the pace of your life.

***

Your senses are part of your ***emotional imprints***. You've had a memory or emotion evoked by a smell or a sound. Whether you are conscious of it or not your body and mind remember everything you have lived through from your conception to the present. We record our experiences. This means you have ***emotional imprints*** that you are not aware of, yet which affect you. You absorb information every day. Your senses are a doorway to your internal universe. The more consciously you choose what you take in the more you are determining how you live. This is not to say that by focusing only on beauty you will be free from suffering. You won't. Suffering is part of human existence. It does mean, however, that you can choose not to poison yourself. You don't have to invite horror into your life. Life will provide plenty of challenges and opportunities to experience and learn.

There are times when the suffering and horrors of this planet enter our lives and we need to deal with them. Allowing yourself to respond from the heart to what your senses bring you is being alive. When presented with pain, feel your pain. When presented with joy, feel your joy. Feeling from your depths is creative. It requires that you be in the present. When you allow yourself to feel fully then you are giving yourself permission to participate in life.

There is a constant flow of information into the psyche of an Internet user. It is important to interrupt this periodically. Take time regularly to leave your computer and encounter natural beauty. You will enrich your life.

6.
Joy

Happiness, pleasure, good feelings; it feels good to feel good!

We all find joy in different places. For me the ultimate pleasure is lying in the hot sun on an ocean beach, feeling the breeze, hearing the sounds of the ocean and wind, relaxing. That is ecstasy to me.

What brings you joy? Do you take time away from your computer to do non-cyber things?

Awareness of Joy

Remember a time of joy from your past. Where were you? Who was there? What felt so good? Remember in detail what you saw, heard, tasted, smelled, felt on your skin. Bring back some of that feeling by remembering it.

Imagine doing a happy dance or making joyful sounds. What would they be like? Try it right now! Let joyful feelings move your body, come out in a sound, even if you're someone who doesn't usually do something like this. If you're not willing to do it, visualize your happy dance in your mind, imagine your joyful sounds.

Check in with your feelings again.

Love   Joy   Anger   Sadness   Fear

Did you give yourself permission to feel joy? If no, what was the barrier? What are the *emotional imprints* which were activated?

Were you breathing fully?

Do you know someone who allows themself to feel and express joy? Do you know anyone who doesn't?

Were people in your family joyful? How did they show it? How did they stop themselves from showing it?

If you had total permission to express your joy what would you do?

***

If it were always sunny and never rained we would have a drought. If it always rained we would be flooded. The same is true with our feelings. The person who seeks to be happy all the time, to feel no pain, is barking up the wrong tree. Life doesn't work that way. We must learn to accept our feelings of discomfort along with our feelings of pleasure or we are not living, we are pretending to live. There needs to be balance for us to be emotionally healthy.

I went to Hawaii with my friend Maryann for 2 weeks in August 1977, right before I was to start at Goddard College. We spent our first night on a piece of beach on the side of the road halfway between Lihuie and Hanalei on the island of Kauai. We didn't know where we were headed. We hadn't planned where to stay or how to get around. We figured we could sleep on beaches, hitch rides, and that everything would be fine. We were seeking total bliss.

When we awoke the next morning we headed north. We found a little store run by Hare Krishnas who allowed us to leave our backpacks in their store room. We hitch-hiked further north taking with us only our money, airline tickets, and sleeping bags. We explored beaches, ate mangoes, papayas, and pineapples. The sun was hot, the sky was clear, we were in paradise. Evening came and we found a state campground. We decided not to pay the fee to stay there. We were thinking "Hey man everything's cool...we're special...WE don't have to pay." We slept in the woods next to the campground.

The next morning we used the campground facilities to shower and brush our teeth. We returned to our campsite to find that our stuff was gone. Stolen! Someone had ripped us off and we were indignant! They had stolen our money and our airplane tickets.

*Instant karma. We'd stolen the use of the camp facilities and paid a price for it. We were out of balance, and we were brought into balance by being ripped off. We were intent on **only** having a good time and we didn't consider taking responsibility, paying for use of the campground, being in balance. Our dream became a nightmare.*

Consider the need to balance out the control you have in the cyber world with the lack of control the "real world" presents us with. The challenges offered by difficult situations are part of how we learn. Without them we would stagnate. Choosing cyberspace over "real life" will inevitably backfire because there is no balance in that choice.

Joy feels good. People like it. There are, however, people who learn to avoid pleasure or joy because it has become associated with abuse or danger. An example of this is when people are sexually abused. The combination of sexual stimulation which can evoke pleasure, combined with invasion and danger, creates an **emotional imprint** which may lead to avoidance of pleasure. Another example is a child who both loves and fears its abuser. It learns to fear the positive things it receives from the abuser because abuse inevitably follows. It is possible for people who have been abused to experience healing. This requires focused introspection, usually with help from a counselor and/or friends, family and community. This process is not easy. It can be painful and take a long time. It is enriching, though, and leads to profound change.

People seek happiness. Many people who go to therapists or healers say "I want to feel good. I want to be happy." They seek relationships which make them happy, experiences which bring pleasure. This is well and good except when the person is seeking joy and pleasure to the exclusion of other feelings. The more one avoids a thing the more it is present in one's life. Seek to avoid grief and you will find grief, for in seeking to avoid something you reinforce your attachment to that very thing.

You can spend hours online avoiding things in life. Being in cyberspace offers you the illusion of control. You decide who to talk with, what you see, where you go. Your experience online is disembodied, so when you turn off the computer there you are with your life to deal with. If you are running from life into cyberspace, stop and look at that. Are there feelings you are trying to avoid?

Joy can be present within feelings of fear, sadness and anger. Allow yourself to integrate and balance your feelings rather than seek to feel only one way. There is aliveness in feeling grief, fear, or anger. It's good to feel your feelings.

I was body surfing while on Kauai. A huge wave, probably 15 feet tall, swept over me, and I knew I was in trouble. I was scared. The wave crashed over me and drove me to the sandy bottom, twisting my spine and cracking a vertebrae in my neck. I couldn't resist the wave. It was too strong. If I resisted I would have been broken. I surrendered. It wasn't a conscious decision, my survival instincts took over. I was washed up on the shore, winded, in pain, frightened. I was injured, but less than I might have been. If I'd have gone rigid the wave would have broken my back and I probably would have been killed. Surrender or die; I surrendered.

The physical injuries I sustained on Kauai (a cracked vertebra in my neck and twisted lumbar spine) changed my life. I was in pain for years and my mission became to heal myself. My neck and shoulders hurt. I had sciatica down both legs full force for months at a time over a six year period. Sometimes I cried thinking that I couldn't stand anymore, and the crying helped some. I tried Rolfing, massage, psychotherapy, primal therapy, dance therapy, and as I experienced each therapy I learned. I became a Massage Therapist. I saw that the physiological and the emotional were connected in my own pain and thought it must be so with others too, so I become a Psychotherapist. At age 25 I finally accepted that I was gay after struggling with my sexual orientation for my entire adolescence. I had been numbing the pain in my body and the pain of denying who I was, self-medicating with marijuana. I gave up smoking pot and "came out" within weeks of each other.

My search for healing brought me to embrace the alchemy of life and led me to great joy, sometimes through great pain. Accepting pain, being willing to feel it in order to decipher it, was hard to do but ultimately led me in a positive direction. Discomfort has taught me that I am more than my body, that I am spiritual, and that all of us are more than just physical creatures. I realized that I could learn and grow and choose where to focus my attention. I learned to treat my body differently. I learned how to stand and walk so that gravity and I were working together rather than fighting, pulling my muscles and bones in different directions. I got involved with Yoga as a daily practice. Yoga nourishes physically, mentally and spiritually. I learned about my ability to connect psychically and spiritually with others. I learned to participate in groups of many kinds, to experience nature more deeply and to participate in the healing of others; all things of great joy in my life.

Joy can be found in unexpected places. Each moment is an opportunity to feel joy in your own aliveness. Take time to stop and be present in this moment.

7.
Sadness

Sorrow is deep and passionate, yet sometimes people attempt to avoid sadness and grief. Being "unhappy" is scorned, looked down upon. We are encouraged to "lighten up" or "just be happy."

Have you ever tried to avoid feeling sad? Did it work? Have you ever had someone try to make you feel better when what you needed was for them to listen, empathize and accept you?

Working as a psychotherapist often involves dealing with sad feelings. Many people share their grief with me. Here are a couple of the most common things people have wanted from me when they are feeling sad:

1) to get out of the way of their sadness,to step aside and let it flow (offer acceptance).

2) to be "with" the person without trying to "fix" anything (empathy).

People will go to great lengths to avoid feeling sad. Spending tons of time in cyberspace is just one method.

This dance of denial ironically leads to more sadness. Avoidance of any feeling makes that feeling stay with you until it is felt and allowed to pass through you, or until it gets buried within your psyche and body, possibly manifesting as physical symptoms and illness.

Sadness, like other feelings, exists on a spectrum. From a mild case of the blues to overwhelming grief, sadness can feel like a wave washing over you, invoking the fear of drowning. People have told me "I am afraid if I start crying I'll never stop." I know that when I've cried enough I release something and that makes space for other feelings.

A woman came to me who hadn't cried in 40 years. She cried continuously for the first 6 months of her therapy. Eventually the tears became occasional, as they do for most people. Her life was not miraculously transformed into everything she wanted but she was no longer carrying an ocean of uncried tears. She had space to experience other feelings and new relationships.

When I was 15, the autumn after my father died, I went back to Vermont to Shaker Mountain School. There was a new staff member. He was in his early 20's. A real "guy." I fell completely in love. I knew I was gay, and wasn't dealing with it, but I felt strongly toward this person. At the same time I knew he could never love me. I felt ugly and clumsy. I wasn't physically daring, I was afraid of getting hurt. I couldn't play an instrument. I was an awkward adolescent male with yearnings which I thought were disgusting. How could anyone, least of all this beautiful man, love me? The grief was overwhelming. I cried a lot. I smoked a lot of pot. I didn't tell anyone how I felt. The sadness of losing my father, and the pain of unrequited love, compounded my pain. I had no compassion for myself. I was often in despair.

Life brings pain and sadness to us all. Either it breaks us or we grow stronger from it. Life brings change which we often experience as loss. Change is inevitable. Relationships, situations, possessions and feelings all come and go. Change is part of the ebb and flow of life. Sometimes however, we find we want desperately to hold on to something, someone, some feeling. We grip tightly, literally, figuratively, and create tension. We don't want to feel loss but we must. We can combine those feelings with compassion and heal.

Notice that in holding on tightly we have already lost what we are holding onto. It has become a new experience, that of holding on. By trying to avoid loss we have created loss. It is possible to learn to recognize the feelings which accompany loss as growing pains and to accept them rather than cling to them desperately. We need to cling to and feel our desperation sometimes, that's part of life. Loss is a form of change, and change is inevitable. There is no real loss in the universe. The law of conservation of energy states that matter can neither be created nor destroyed.

Sometimes I feel deep grief. I don't always know what it's about. The feeling is strong and tender. I breathe into it, feel it as deeply as I can. I nourish myself by accepting the feeling. There is self love in accepting my sadness, compassion for myself and others. By crying and feeling sad I am washed clean. I surrender to the futility of trying to control life. I accept the flow of grief and allow it to carry me. I am released, refreshed, and made ready for the next experience.

The human species is an organism made up of many cells. We are evolving, becoming a conscious entity, moving toward peace, learning to act with compassion and respect for the planet and all life forms. I hope that some day humankind will be that healthy.

I hear the news about another bombing, another torture, another rape, another beating. I feel sadness to my core. I sob. I grieve. I release. I am a vent for the grief of our

Relax into sadness, allow it to wash through you. Surrender gives your mind release from **emotional imprints** and allows your body to learn peace with what is so.

We often try to run from sadness by being busy, afraid that if we stop moving, the grief will be more than we can bear. Eventually we must either stop and feel or become ill from stress.

Sometimes I feel overfilled with grief. I can't stand anymore. But I go to my office and listen. People spill their guts about painful childhood, trauma, rejection, self loathing, needing to feel whole and loved. I cry all the way home and feel a sense of relief. I am nourished being with people as they heal, and by my release of emotion.

Aware of Sadness

Find your sadness. Feel the sensations sadness brings into your body. Feel what's behind your eyes, in your face.

Are you remembering the past or are you grieving something in the present?

Feel it. Embrace it. Breathe it in. Let it move through you. Notice any tensing of your body, breathe into it and let it go.

Is there anything you want another person to know about your feelings? Who do you want to share your sadness with? Can you feel aliveness in your grief?

When you are engaged online what is happening with your feelings? Are you aware of them? Do you seek to be aware of them? Do you seek to avoid them? Have you had emotional experiences online?

***

The cyber environment lends itself easily to a numbing of emotions. It is not necessary to become numb. If you choose to focus on your emotions regularly, to stop what you are doing and breathe, then you will not become numb. All of your feelings are gifts to you whether you enjoy them or not. Feeling your feelings, not becoming numb, is an integral part of emotional and physical wellness.

8.
Anger

I've heard some people say that anger isn't a real feeling at all but a bridge between love and fear, is pure animal aggression which must be eliminated, isn't spiritual. I believe anger is an instinctual response to the perceived threat to one's safety or the safety of a loved one. The impulse is to protect, often by lashing out.

Anger is considered a "bad" emotion in our culture, but it isn't "bad." It's part of healthy emotional balance. The keys to healthy anger are clear parameters about what behavior is acceptable, and our willingness to look at our ***emotional imprints*** and take responsibility for them. We experience degrees of anger, from minor annoyance to white hot rage. When your anger seems out of proportion to what is happening, that is an activated ***emotional imprint***.

It is important to feel anger. Anger offers the opportunity to learn. Anger demands recognition and expression or it builds as tension in the body and can lead to emotional problems and physical illness. It's not healthy to give anger unlimited expression, but it's also not healthy to keep anger completely hidden or denied.

Some people are afraid of their anger. They feel that their rage could decimate cities if unleashed. We know that won't really happen. We are not omnipotent, and our anger, no matter how strong or how deep, is just a feeling. Even so, people often fear their anger.

It is appropriate to practice restraint with your violent feelings. Fear of violence is healthy. Violence is the acting out of rage in hurtful ways. However, there are ways to express anger physically which are safe, like using a punching bag. That's different from acting your anger out on people. Knowing the difference between feeling/expressing your anger and acting it out is important. Feeling and releasing anger through safe, authentic expression is very beneficial. Anger held inside and never expressed can build into a destructive force and lead to acting out on other people or on one's self. Physical illness resulting from unexpressed emotion is a form of acting out.

The words "violence" and "violation" are kin. These behaviors are not harmonious. Remember our universal particles vibrating? In violence the particles are moving and vibrating in ways which are out of harmony. The thoughts and ensuing actions are not harmonious. Think of the sounds of violence. They are discordant, not harmonious.

We know that particles exposed to one another begin to influence each other, to vibrate in resonance with each other. Consider tuning forks. Strike one tuning fork and hold it near another and the second one will start to vibrate, picking up on the vibrations of the first tuning fork. The same is true with people. People try to connect with each other when their **emotional imprints** aren't in the way. Think about "contagious moods." It may be a challenge to accept this when you think about world events, but people are attracted to harmony.

Exposure to violence can set up a chain reaction, like a set of dominoes lined up and set in motion. Your resonant energy field, the particles which constitute your body, are affected. Your rate of vibration is altered by the vibrations of the violence. If you have ever been in a violent situation you know what I mean. You felt different after the experience, and it took time for you to recover, to get back to the more harmonious state of vibration you were in before the violence occurred. Some people have been exposed to violence of such intensity, and at such close proximity, that their energy field resonates with the violence for a long time.

I worked at a Vietnam Veteran's Counseling Center as an intern for 9 months. I saw that the men and women who had served in the war had been so affected by exposure to violence that even though it had been years, decades for some, they were still trying to recover from it. The psychological diagnosis is Post Traumatic Stress Disorder (PTSD). I have seen the same thing in people who have been raped, sexually abused, beaten, or otherwise violated. Any life threatening trauma will do it; auto accident, mugging, etc. The vibrations can take someone so far from their original harmonious state that there is intense need to focus on expressing the feelings so there can be healing. Sometimes this takes years. Sometimes the healing is partial, thus the term "walking wounded."

Violent behavior is a form of communication. It is the acting out of something which the person has in their psyche. A whole country can act out something in it's collective psyche. That's what war is. A person expresses anger, fear and grief through acts of violence, and the people who are violated feel, to some degree, what the violator feels; the anger, fear, grief. Rather than facilitating healing, as conscious non-violent communication could, the violent exchange serves only to perpetuate the distress which began the violence in the first place, adding momentum to it. The one who is violated then carries the distress. Unless they heal themselves they may pass it on to someone else. The abused may become an abuser, or s/he may go into the world and act out their pain in ways which affect others, or they may act out upon themself. Think of people in traffic displaying hostility, acting out their distress. The anger can be passed from one person to another. I've done it. Have you? There have also been days when I observed the automobile wars without participating. I wasn't "tuned into" the vibrations of hostility.

There are people who intentionally act out, communicating their distress, passing it on to others. They are wounded and altered by what has happened to them in such a way that they need to let others know what it's like for them. They choose to pass it on out of revenge. These are the people we sometimes refer to as "sociopaths."

Anger can put things into perspective. I have found empowerment in anger, affirming my sense of justice. Feeling angry about injustice or disappointment has allowed me to clarify what my values are.

I was coordinating a workshop for 65 teens. We had a staff of 25 teens and adults together for a week. The safety and intimacy in the group was strong and very sweet. During a staff meeting a highly charged issue relating to the sexual behavior of a young person in the organization (who was not present at this workshop) came up. What I perceived as agency politics and denial about this issue from the Directors, enraged me.

When an agency representative came to the workshop the next day I expressed myself to him. I felt anger surging through my body. I shook. I felt as if I had been plugged into the earth and sky . I was not abusive but I was loud. I told the agency representative what had come up in the staff meeting, how I felt, and what I wanted to happen with regards to the issue. This was a satisfying experience of anger. Part of what was satisfying was that the man from the agency stood his ground and listened. He didn't react. He didn't defend. He didn't try to stop me. He received my anger. It was a great gift he gave me.

Awareness of Anger

Remember a time when you felt angry. How did your body feel? What were your thoughts? Did you feel safe with your anger? Did you let anyone know you were angry? How?

Remember when you witnessed someone expressing anger. What was that like for you emotionally? Did you feel safe?

How did people deal with anger in your family? Did they express it or hold it in? Did they blame others for their anger or did they take responsibility for it?

Check in with your emotions.

Love   Joy   Anger   Sadness   Fear

How do you feel about yourself when you are angry?

What are your beliefs about anger? Is anger good? Is it bad? Can it be constructive?

Do you have permission to explore your anger? To what extent?

Do you notice any *emotional imprints* connected with anger?

If you were to make a really angry sound, what would it be?

Do you have any old anger that you are holding on to?

Do you have any anger you have been avoiding, or are afraid to explore?

***

Are you someone who runs from anger? If you are, where do you run to? You probably encounter your anger even as you try to avoid it. If being "in your head" is a method you employ to avoid a feeling then being online offers the perfect escape from uncomfortable emotions. All feelings have a body-awareness component. When we are willing to delve into the emotional, then we are opening ourselves, literally, to the universe. Remember that emotion is a quantum event. Being open to the universe, not fighting the wave, allows you to grow and sometimes is the only way to survive. Time spent online can take you out of your body and emotions. Remember, check in with yourself often about how you're feeling, and whether you need to express or otherwise deal with any feelings. Be aware of your angry feelings, learn from them, deal with them constructively. You will grow from the experience.

9.
Love

A Three Part Dream

I go to a workshop preview. First we are shown a video tape of the last group who attended. They are shrieking and hitting one another in anger and fear.

I decide to do the workshop.

There is a cardboard box on a table beside the door inside the training room. There are three Martians in the box. They are green creatures about 14 inches tall. They are covered with felt-like fur. The workshop participants, of which I am one, don't interact with them, but they are there and they are the source of the workshop material.

The teacher is a tall man with dark hair and a kind face. We come to a point in the workshop where suddenly everybody starts hitting the person on the other side of the person they are next to. The explanation for this is that we love the one we are next to and don't want to hurt them, so we hit the others. Then we start shrieking. I remember the video.

We stop hitting and shrieking and look at each other and the room is filled with love. The choice is made. We choose love. It happens very suddenly just as the hitting happened suddenly. It's powerful and beautiful and simple. As we leave the workshop I stop and thank the Martians in the box. They look at me sweetly.

After the workshop there is a dinner being held for us in a large sunlit dining room. We are all beaming. I go to sit in the BIG chair, the seat of power, of honor. I seek that position. I sit in the chair. Then I see that someone else is in the real seat of power and honor across the table, someone who is not seeking either. I realize that I don't need to sit where I have chosen. Seeking power gives me false power. It isolates me. I go and sit with my friends. There is a time of group hugging. I make eye contact with people. It is very loving and beautiful.

We are in New York City after the workshop and the dinner. It is a sunny day, very bright. There are lots of people on the sidewalks. It is a festival! I catch glimpses of my friends. I feel a new feeling about all the people on the street; loving them, seeing them as not yet having made the choice to love, as we did in the workshop. I go into a Jewish store which sells mostly palm fronds but also candy. I have 4 quarters. I get 2 big chocolate *strawberry creams for $.49 each. An old woman is talking on and on. I excuse myself, pay the man behind the counter. I give my chocolates to the old woman and go back out onto the street. I feel lost. Where are my brothers and sisters, friends from the workshop? I hear them calling me from far away. They are in the middle of a huge grassy park. There is a wide avenue between me and the park with lots of traffic and I remember, I can choose love! I remember that love is an actual substance which we are surrounded by and suffused with, and as I focus on love I slowly lift off the ground, over the avenue through the air. I float gradually higher and higher as I get close to my friends. I am focused on love and that allows me to fly! I get to where my friends are and we are celebrating!*

This dream was powerful. It changed me. When I woke up after dreaming I "saw" love as an actual substance which exists in the world, suffusing everything. The martians were teaching love to the workshop partici-pants. I experienced clarity about false power and real power; the difference between seeking importance, which is isolating, and finding true power in connection. The scene in the park showed me that we live in an ocean of love, and remembering this makes all things are possible. Awareness of love clarifies issues of power, connection, and offers a sense of possibility.

Love is the basis of our emotional and spiritual lives, both the presence and absence of love. We want to love and feel loved. Love means different things to different people. How can someone show their love to you? How do you love? How do we tap into love, share it, experience it?

There are many different loves in our lives; love of partner, child, friend, love of self, love of creation, love of creator. All come from the same place within us. You can feel where love comes from when you are loving. The desire to be truly known and accepted is a primary urge for most people. Relationships which involve love change people. Love creates growth.

We live our lives, learn our lessons and are **emotionally imprinted** with unique patterns. We share the capacity for and the need to love. The absence of loving leaves a painful gap. It is important to allow ourselves to feel the pain rather than to avoid it. Feeling leads to healing which allows us to give and receive love again.

A Dream

I dreamt I was with Roseanne (the actress/comedian). I dream about her occasionally. I like what I know of her. She's funny, irreverent, and determined to speak her truth no matter how she's received. We were having a conversation. I touched a piece of wood and my hand melted into the wood. I was doing this to demonstrate lack of separation with the universe. I told her the universe loved her because she is the universe, that though she'd felt pain in her life, I knew she had always loved the universe, for that is the universe loving itself. I then put my hand through a wall. I could have walked through the wall but I'd made my point to her and to myself. I am the universe. I am not separate from anything or anyone, and neither is Roseanne.

I awoke from this dream feeling loved and loving. The experience was one of oneness with the universe, not experiencing physical limitation but unity instead, and sharing this with Roseanne.

Awareness of Love

Remember someone who loves you. How does their love effect your life? How do they let you know that they love you?

Think of someone you love. How do you want your love to affect their life? How do you demonstrate your love?

Can you feel love right now?

How did people in your childhood demonstrate love for each other? Did anyone withhold love from you during your childhood?

Notice your reactions to these questions. Breathe and check in with your feelings.

Love   Joy   Anger   Sadness   Fear

Do you feel love in your body?

Do you see yourself as a loving person?

Do you have permission to be loving?

Are you ever afraid to love? Do you ever love secretly without sharing?

What are your ***emotional imprints*** about love?

Breathe deeply. Say the word aloud to yourself slowly a few times. Love.

What do you notice?

***

Love / 74

You can evoke loving feelings by thinking of someone you love, or by focusing on the oneness of the universe and your part in it. Choose to focus on love every day of your life. Love is a source of energy and renewal, a wonderful lens through which to see the world. Focusing on love changes you.

We often hear about self-esteem but what it is? Liking what you see in the mirror? Feeling good about what you do? What about self love? Self-esteem and self-love are different. Loving yourself is feeling love for the person you are. Self-esteem is more about approving of your-self based on what you do. Both are important and valuable. The more deeply you love yourself and see value in your contributions to the world the more open you will be to the love of others. Do you look at yourself with loving eyes?

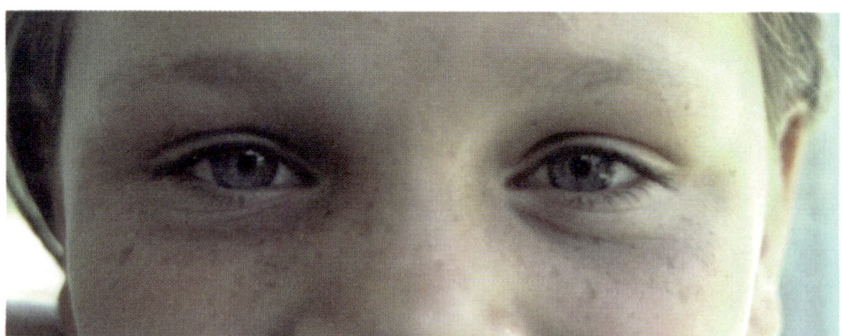

How do you regard yourself? Do you feel differently about yourself at different times? Is the way you feel about yourself impacted in any way by your time online?

One definition of addiction is that "you have a problem with (alcohol, drugs, sex, being online) if any relationship in your life is negatively impacted by that involvement." I believe that addiction is directly connected to not feeling loving towards one's self, but feeling instead an emptiness that one attempts to fill with the addictive behavior.

Do you love yourself?

10.
Multiple Personae

People create multiple personae online to explore themselves. People experiment with different genders or names. The online medium lends itself to exper-imenting with parts of yourself you don't feel safe exploring "in real life." You can be any age, any gender, any physique, any race, any sexuality.

In therapy we sometimes talk about "parts." The inner child, the inner male for females or inner female for males, and other "parts." Any identity you imagine can exist inside you. Cyberspace allows people to bring their hidden unexplored inner personae out into the world to interact with others.

In the chat room called "The Refuge" there was a guy in his early 20's who was popular among the room regulars. He introduced an older male couple and a young woman to the room, and they became frequent visitors. Soon it became clear that all these were one person. S/ he (we never knew for sure) was acting out something by being all these people. The "roomies" were very angry. The culture of the room was based on trust and the trust had been breached. Even in a virtual community, trust

*is the basis for relationship. This event was the begin-
ning of the end of The Refuge. I wonder who those
multiple personae belonged to and what that person was
exploring?*

There can be immense psychological value in exploring
various aspects of self. We do it in psychotherapy with
a variety of techniques: Gestalt, Inner Dialogue, Psycho-
drama. Jungian psychology is replete with exploration
and integration of anima and animus, the male's female
essence and the female's male essence. In cyberspace
when people are being different "selves" they are not
necessarily doing it with a conscious healing process in
mind. It can be a great value to explore your multiple
personae[7] with the conscious goal of learning about
yourself and aspects of your personality.

Multiple personae come from secret fantasies, hidden
fears and desires. Often these are of a sexual nature
because our society, despite the so-called sexual revolution, is basically erotophobic. People have sexual fantasies which they suppress because of fear, shame, cultural
disapproval. The freedom to acknowledge one's fantasies can be constrained by fear.

Violent fantasies or fantasies involving children are
socially unacceptable because they cause suffering in

others and we do not accept them as valid personal expression. These fantasies are not as unusual as our societal conventions would have us believe. Many people have them.

The value of exploring fantasies and multiple personae is that as we learn more about ourselves we integrate more of our unconscious selves into our conscious awareness. This integration opens up creativity. Creativity in art, music, writing, dance etc., all come from the willingness to imagine and give expression to our imaginings.

The danger in playing with multiple personae is that you can reinforce whatever feelings of fragmentation and incongruence exist between your inner and outer worlds. Role playing on or offline can serve to drive apart rather than bring together different aspects of your personality. This is especially true if fear is present and you cannot or do not face your fear. This leads to disconnection from people and spirituality.

We tend to internalize various archetypal personae, like the mother, the father, the lover. We also have our own unique characters inside us. Are you interested in meeting some of yours?

Personae Awareness

Breathe and relax. Ask yourself for some of the personae or characters inside you to come forth. Imagine who might be in there. Allow the characters to come forth just as any imaginings can come forth. Did you ever play-act as a child? What characters did you play with then? What play characters exist inside you to play with now? Notice what/who comes forward.

How are you reacting to them? Do you like who's there? How do you feel about them? Are you willing to have a conversation with the different characters inside you?

How are your various selves feeling?

Love   Joy   Anger   Sadness   Fear

Did you experience any other feelings?

Have you known about these parts of you?

Can you accept the personae you encountered? Do they challenge your self concept? How?

What can you learn about yourself by including these inner characters?

Are these parts of yourself always inside or do you ever let them out?

Go for a walk and take some or all of your inner characters with you. Dialogue with them consciously as you experience the outside world. Write about this experience, or share it with a friend.

***

Have you explored being different people in cyberspace? What was it like? If you haven't, what do you think of the idea? I am not suggesting that you need to do this, but I am asking you to consider whether you allow as much of yourself as possible to be part of your "usual" self. One way to explore this is to become aware of a persona that is not integrated into your "usual" self. What comes to mind as you consider that idea? What aspects of yourself are kept hidden? Do you have questions about why parts of you are hidden? Are there parts of yourself that you would like to integrate more? How can you do this?

The more we know ourselves, the more we are able to share. Some of our inner selves may be best kept inside, like fantasies that don't need to be acted out. Some may encourage creativity and our sense of connection.

11.
Sex

Sex is a part of life where you can be open to yourself and to another. Intimate sexual relating includes dropping barriers, an assumption of safety which in turn can lead to healing. It can also lead to injury. Healing through sex can happen when there is a deepening of self. Wounding can happen if there is dishonesty or exploitation, if trust is breached.

In cyberspace people can explore their sexuality in the safety of anonymity. Exploring what has been hidden, and perhaps has been a source of shame, can be pro-foundly liberating, a coming out of shadows and into light. When part of you is hidden in shadows and you come to terms with it and accept it, then you are enriched.

I am not advocating acting out all of your repressed impulses, but becoming more aware of what is inside you and responding to yourself with love.

The downside of the cyber-sexual revolution is the potential for addiction. Any time you explore something pleasurable and taboo you enter a forbidden zone. Tell a kid they can't have sugar and the odds are when they

have the opportunity they will overindulge. Online,
explore the chat rooms and you'll find indulgence and
over indulgence of sexual fantasies, which can be habit
forming, especially if a person has gaps in his/her life, or
feelings they are not facing.

Sex is where animal, emotional, and spiritual natures
can meet. Sex has the potential to include basic lust and
deep soul connection, and everything in between. The
possibilities are infinite. Unfortunately many societies
(religions, nations, relationships) have been organized
along principles antithetical to sex and what it repre-
sents. These societies are hierarchical, demanding
conformity, discouraging heterogeneous creativity.
Growing up with this indoctrination leads many to
repress their native passions, including sexuality. Capi-
talism celebrates material gain over creativity, and talent
is often viewed as a commodity. This leads to a world
view which turns sex into a commodity for consumption
rather than a place of healing, connection and pleasure.

Sex is a doorway for creativity. You can delve into
spontaneous passion with your partner (or yourself)
through love making. Whole self sex has a wild quality,
not tamed by inhibitions. Imagine a Zebra wondering if

it is "good enough". Yet we often wonder if we are attractive enough, or "good enough" sexually.

What is the essence of your sexuality? Your passion is part of your nature. How would you express your passion if you felt completely free to be yourself? Imagine your sexual passion as an animal, or another natural phenomenon. What do you imagine?

Do you feel great about your sexuality? Do you feel bad? How did you come to feel this way? What life events brought you to this point? What choices did other people make which have affected your sexuality? What choices have you made? What is your sexual nature? Notice your thoughts, feelings, and body as you explore these questions. By doing so you can learn about what lies hidden within your psyche, your beliefs and the emotional imprints you carry around about your sexuality.

Have you ever wanted to be sexual with someone but thought it was wrong? If you are engaged in concensual sex with a peer should any sexual expression be taboo? Many religions teach that sex is sacred only if it is for reproduction, and that we must suppress our desires. Is this part of your religious background? How has religion affected your beliefs about yourself sexually?

Have you ever been sexual with someone you didn't want to be with, or when you didn't want to be sexual? Have you ever been pressured into being sexual or pressured someone else? Have you ever been sexual in a way which wasted your energy? How are issues of power part of your sexuality?

Sexuality Awareness

Remember the first time you had sex with another person. Recall the place, the person, how you felt. Remember the sounds, smells, tastes, skin sensations. Were you ***emotionally imprinted*** by this experience?

Think of your most recent sexual experience. Remember the place, the person, how you felt in your skin and in your feelings. Does this remind you of your first experience in any way? What's different? What's similar?

Think of one sexual fantasy you like. Do you have any judgments about it? Does it refer back to your first sexual experience?

What emotions come up for you with this awareness?

Love   Joy   Anger   Sadness   Fear

Do you experience sexual sensations mainly in your genitals or in other parts of your body as well?

Do you consider yourself a sexual person? Do you think others see you as you see yourself?

Do you give yourself permission to be sexually fulfilled or is there a lid on your sexuality?

What are your *emotional imprints* about sex? What would you like to express sexually that you don't?

***

Humans are hard-wired for sex for reproduction and pleasure. We receive *emotional imprinting* about sex (and about ourselves as sexual beings) from our environment and our experiences. Acknowledging how we are imprinted is part of healing any wounds we might have about sex, and deepening our sexual self.

Evidence is mounting which indicates that sexual orientation is part of our physiology as well as our psychology[8]. This implies that the cultural taboos about homosexuality and bisexuality are based on fears which have been handed down for centuries through cultural institutions i.e., religion, family, political and economic structures. The standards of heterosexuality and patriarchy have been central in forming contemporary society, how people live and treat one another. These forms have inculcated prejudice and fear by imbuing people with expectations, values, and *emotional imprints* which do not reflect the full human potential.

There is a difference between sexual orientation and sexual preference. We develop personal preferences based upon *emotional imprinting*, our bodies, and many other stimuli, but sexual orientation appears to be biological. Many people I have talked with say that they are basically bisexual with predominant interests in either hetero- or homo- sexuality. Some have said they are exclusively one or the other in behavior but have feelings of bisexuality, and some people have said that they only have homo- or hetero- erotic feelings.

I spent much of my life keeping a lid on my sexuality. When I was 35 I took the lid off the pot! I stopped looking at monogamy as a moral issue, which is how I had been brought up to see it, and started to see monogamy as a relational issue. Choosing one partner is wonderful when it's what you want, but it's OK if it isn't what you want. This insight allowed me to experience sex differently. I explored fantasies. I had fun. I explored. As a result I began shedding the belief that I was ugly. I touched and I was touched. I explored connections which were not romantic but were meaningful. I also made mistakes. I had sexual contact out of feelings of obligation. I had spent years repressing sexual desire because I had not given myself permission to explore. I finally dipped into the well of unexplored fantasy in cyberspace. With the anonymity of cyberspace I felt free to explore my sexuality. I found it liberating. My creativity became more alive, my appreciation of my body changed and became greater.

Lots of people are exploring their sexuality in cyberspace, freeing energy that has been bound. Societal conventions cause many people to feel stifled. Some seek to explore bisexuality, sexual power dynamics, different roles, different partners, in cyberspace. This has the potential to reduce sex to a level of pure objectification due, in part, to the one-dimensionality of the online medium. It can also allow exploration of desires which have been feared or forbidden. Many people have found themselves exploring their repressed eroticism in cyberspace. This is a double edged sword; cutting bonds that restrict, but also potentially cutting bonds of connection that exist offline.

Sexuality Without Shame

Imagine living without shame. How would you be different? Think about your sexual relationship(s). What are your expectations of sex? What do you want from sex? In your present sexual relating are you in a role? Did you chose that consciously? Do you give or withhold sexually? Does your partner? How did you and your partner create the sexual culture of the relationship? Did you discuss it overtly?

How do you feel about your body sexually? Consider how you appear, but also how you feel in your body.

Do you limit your sexual expression in any way? How? Why?

What would you do differently if you didn't have limits? How do your limits keep you safe and how do they confine you?

Do you have any fear of sex?

What is the gift of your unique sexuality?

What kind of feelings do these questions stir up?

Love   Joy   Anger   Sadness   Fear

What ***emotional imprints*** are you aware of in connection with your sexuality?

What are your questions about sexuality? Do you ever discuss sex and sexuality with friends?

Are there aspects of your sexuality which you keep hidden even from yourself?

Each of us has to discover for ourselves the meaning of sex in our lives.

***

12.
Body

I've been a Massage/Body Therapist for years. I've touched hundreds, thousands of people. Each person expresses inner beauty and life force through their body. I experience that beauty when I touch them. People come to me when they are hurting or aren't feeling well. I touch them in a way which brings them awareness of their beauty and aliveness. People experience deep relaxation, emotional releasing and release from physical pain.

By addressing my own injuries and healing I've become fascinated with the human body. Complex, simple, many systems co-existing, nurturing each other; I am awed by the human body. You can experience awe in connection with your body.

I ask myself "What food would be best for me now?" and my body tells me. I ask my body for specific awarenesses, like what's happening in a certain organ or body part, I receive the information. If I am experiencing physical pain I say to myself "endorphins please!" and my brain sends endorphins. When you communicate with someone you speak to them and you listen for their response.

The same is possible with your body. You can have a conscious relationship with your body.

Focusing on your computer, just like going to the movies or watching television, steers your awareness out of your body. There is nothing inherently unhealthy about that unless it becomes the status quo, or unless it contributes to your being unable to return to awareness of your body.

Body Awareness

Be aware of your skin. Feel it. Breathe. Feel your skin in contact with the air. Skin breathes. Be aware of your muscles. They are contracting and releasing. Be aware of your bones. There is a skeleton beneath your skin and muscles. Notice your blood vessels bringing nourishment to every cell in your body. Feel your internal organs digesting food, breathing air, pumping and filtering blood. Sense the electrical activity of your nervous system sending electrical impulses fast as light. Feel your brain in your skull; the ultimate biocomputer and more. Breathe deeply and be aware of the life force in your body.

Is it a new experience to practice this kind of body awareness? Do you pay a price for not being aware of your body?

Notice your emotions. Notice your level of acceptance of your body. How are you feeling?

Love   Joy   Anger   Sadness   Fear

Check in with yourself by breathing and asking within. Does your body have a message for you right now? Are you open to receive to it?

Do you have any shame connected with your body?

Are there ways in which you appreciate your body?

How do you care for your body?

What ***emotional imprints*** exist in your body? That's a big question so take your time, notice what answer comes to mind. You might want to ask yourself that question periodically to see what comes to you.

***

Life force is a gift. We all have it and can be aware of it. We can feel the aliveness inside us.

Our bodies are complex; subatomic, atomic, cellular, systemic, etheric, as well as aesthetic, psychological,

93 / Body

relational. I have found that many people feel disconnected from their bodies. They are not aware of their
bodies except as objects. One person said to me "my
body exists to carry my head around." Your body is
much more than that. Your body is your vehicle in this
world, and it is a dynamic living organism which you can
learn from.

Body Appreciation

Look at your hand. See the lines on the skin, the tiny
hairs. Move your fingers. Notice how immediate the
movement is. You *will* it to happen and it does. Bring
your hand close to your face. Smell your scent. Taste
your skin. This amazing hand is part of you! Notice the
blood vessels, bones, joints. Touch your fingernails.
You actually cause them to exist. The life force in you
causes your body to renew itself every moment of every
day, cells reproducing to replace cells which die.

When did you last clip your fingernails? When was your
last haircut? Your nails and hair are growing right now.

You can be aware of your whole body. Take the awareness you've just experienced in your hand, and extend it
into your whole body. Allow your consciousness to fill
your body. Breathe fully and feel your body; alive and

growing, part of the universe. How does this make you feel?

Love   Joy   Anger   Sadness   Fear

Give your body a loving message right now. Tell yourself something that is true about your body that gives you a feeling of being nurtured. Are you willing to do this? Is it easy? Difficult? Impossible? Possible?

When you were a child what beliefs did you form about your body? How did you come to believe those things? How did the adults around you relate to your body? Did they touch you? Did their touch feel good to you?

***

Children discover the world starting with their bodies. Have you watched a child as s/he learned what her/his body can do? Babies play with their feet and genitals, play with your nose and lips. When my little neighbor boy was three he discovered running down the hill behind his house. He called it flying. He still flies down the hill, screaming, smiling, laughing, enjoying his physical existence. His joy in physical existence is part of the discovery of life which he is engaged in. Our bodies are always changing and so there is always more to discover.

95 / Body

Children benefit when they are encouraged to explore and value their bodies.

We didn't play many sports in my family. My father played tennis, but that was the extent to which physical activity was modeled for me at home. At school I played kickball and dodgeball. I climbed on the jungle gym and ran around, swung on the swings. When it came to baseball, football, basketball, I was terrible. I was uncoordinated and I didn't see the appeal in the games anyway. They weren't activities which I'd been taught to value, and I was afraid of getting hurt. Playing rough didn't look like fun to me. I didn't think my body was strong or capable. I started to dislike my body. It was different. I was different. I didn't fit in. It was my body's fault.

Since the Internet is not a physical experience, and we are striving for balance in our lives, it follows that we need to nurture our bodies through awareness.

We have expectations of our bodies, our strengths, our abilities, our looks. We measure and compare those attributes according to standards which come from our families, our immediate surroundings and society. It's important to question the standards you've learned to accept. What are your expectations of your body? Are they good for you? Do they set you up for failure or success? If you could change any of your expectations what would you change?

Acceptance of our bodies is a form of self-love. Our bodies are magnificent. There may be things you want to change, but examine your motives. Wanting to lose or gain weight for your health can makes sense. Wanting to (most likely) lose weight so that you'll resemble the models in magazines comes from an ***emotional imprint*** and requires examination and healing. Appearance is an enormous issue in our society, and deeply involved with sexual politics. We are "supposed" to look a certain way in order to fit into the mold of beauty we've been taught to value. Self acceptance is crucial for healing because if we are not accepting of ourselves then we are not loving ourselves. Self-love motivates good self-care and focus on healing. Healing is the key to a life that gets better and better.

Fitting into someone else's expectations is not about self acceptance or healing. When we are focused on someone else's approval rather than our own, we are giving away our power and our sense of connection with the universe, and defining ourselves by someone else's priorities.

What do you put into your body? What do you eat and drink? You breathe the air which is available where you live. Have you ever smoked, ingested alcohol, taken drugs? How did these things affect you? I smoked off and on for 22 years. I don't anymore. I found pleasure in the act of smoking, but I could always feel the damage to my lungs. I don't do drugs anymore either. I learned that I can experience amazing altered states without the drugs. I also came to the conclusion that putting toxic things into my body was connected to not loving myself.

Halloween 1977. It's THE big party night of the semester. LSD. Pot. Alcohol. Costumes. I feel alienated but I'm trying to have fun anyway. I am dressed as a vampire, I even have cheap temporary caps for my canine teeth so I'll have fangs! We drop acid around 6 o'clock as we are dressing up. I'm painting my fingernails black and wondering if it's the drugs or if I am really feeling the skin under my fingernails suffocate as I paint my nails with these petrochemicals. I feel identified with the dead character I am portraying; isolated in the company of others, toxic, not loved or loving.

Do you receive other's touch? Do you touch others? We need touch. Without it we die. Babies die. Touch is associated with sex, but we also need touch which is sensual, not sexual. Have you ever bruised yourself and had the instinct to hold the part of your body which was in pain? Touch is the oldest form of proactive healing. When a child hurts we hold them. When we bang our toe or our head we hold it. When we are sad or scared, we want to be held. Being online doesn't involve touch.

There are many ways to touch. Touching to give, to soothe, to love.   These touches are very different from touching to hurt, to overpower, to take. The persons being touched can feel the difference even when they cannot let you know it. Touch is another area where *emotional imprinting* plays an important role. The ways in which we are touched as infants and children teach us about how we are received by the world, about relation-ships and safety, our bodies, our value. Babies are, generally, vulnerable and open, unless they have already been traumatized in some way that has caused them to close up. Parents have a lot happening in their lives, and they can unconsciously send messages to their kids which they would rather not be sending. That's part of why it is important for adults to do conscious work on themselves.

Massage is an ancient technique of hands-on healing. There are as many techniques for massage as there are practitioners. I encourage you to find a Therapeutic

Massage practitioner and experience for yourself this sensual healing technique.

Awareness of Touch

Remember the house you grew up in. Accept whatever memory comes to you first.

Who lived there with you? Did you see people touching each other? What kind of touch was it? Did anyone touch you? Did you touch others? What kind of touch do you remember?

Think of your life today, and the presence of touch. Do you see any parallels between your memory and your present life? Are you satisfied with the way touch exists in your life today?

Be aware of your skin. Your skin is sensitive. Touch it. Notice how it feels. Notice your emotional response to your own touch.

Remember any touch which made a lasting impression on you. It could be touch that felt good, or touch that didn't. These memories are important. Your memories allow you to separate impressions of the past from awareness of the present.

Notice your emotions. Notice the sensations in your body. How are you feeling?

Love   Joy   Anger   Sadness   Fear

Are you comfortable touching and being touched? Do you tell people when their touch feels good or doesn't feel good?

Do you ask to be touched when you need or want it? Do you get touched enough? Do you touch other people? Does being online take precedence over being touched?

***

Do you ever feel tense? Sometimes things "get to me" and I feel uptight. At the end of a rough day I can feel tightness in my shoulders and my neck. If it's really been a tough day my lower back might ache. These are my chronic areas stemming in part from the injuries I sustained when bodysurfing in 1977, and partly from ***emotional imprints***. I rarely have these symptoms now, which I attribute to personal awareness and bodywork. I do get them occasionally, and they remind me to pay attention to myself, to stop "doing" and to "be." That tension is a prime example of experiencing feelings in my body. Learning to release tension has been very valuable.

I've received bodywork for many years; Rolfing and Hellerwork series, massage, Contact/Improvisation Dance, muscle group isolation exercises, and Yoga. These are forms of physical attention I choose to give myself. They increase my awareness and sense of health and well being. Through these experiences I've learned things I can do for myself when I feel tense.

Sitting in front of a computer can be very stressful on your body. It is important that you know how to deal with this. The awareness activities you've done in this book have led you deeper into your body. The next activity asks you to work with your awareness to help you release physical tension. This is a new skill; the more you practice, the more accomplished you will become.

Tension Release

This exercise works when you are tense but can give you benefits anytime. Find a place to sit, stand, or lie down. I recommend a private space.

Notice where you feel tension or muscular tightness. Scan from the top of your head down to your toes. Notice tension in your pelvis. Notice your jaw. Notice your spine, the core of your body. (We tend to tense up the tissues around our spinal columns. The tension then moves out from the center effecting other parts of our bodies.)

Deepen your breath. Slow it down. As you deepen your breath begin to relax your pelvic muscles; genitals, sphincters. You may not be able to completely relax these muscles at first. Tighten them and then release and you will find yourself softening your pelvic muscles. Relax the muscles in your jaw. Again tighten them first to feel the release. As you let your pelvis and jaw soften, and breathe fully, you will find tension throughout your body dissipating.

Notice your body and emotions. How are you feeling now?

Love   Joy   Anger   Sadness   Fear

Did you notice emotions or scenarios in your mind which were contributing to your tension?

Did you let go of any tightness? Where in your body was it? How did it feel to do the letting go? Was there any tightness you didn't let go of? Where is it? Do you haveany mental or emotional resistance to letting it go? Are you aware when you tighten your body? Are you aware of what things in your life stimulate you to tenseup? How does being online affect your body?

Is there anything you want to change about the tension patterns in your life?

***

Your relationship with your body is lifelong and determines much of the quality of your existence. You affect your body by how you pay attention to it. If you ignore your body, focusing mainly on your mental experiences, you will eventually receive messages from your body, calls for attention. Don't wait for illness or infirmity, get into your body now! Love and appreciate your physical form and you will reap the benefits.

13.

Food

I love food! I love the variety; different tastes and textures. What is your relationship to food? Do you eat for nutrition, taste, emotional reasons, entertainment? Food provides all of these, and they are all appropriate. Problems arise when we go to extremes. Balance and awareness in our relationship with food, as in the rest of our lives, allows us to be healthy.

Has your relationship with food changed since you began to spend time in cyberspace? Do you eat different foods? Do you eat with more or less attentiveness? How about the speed with which you eat, has that changed? Do you see a healthy or an unhealthy trend?

Popular culture in the United States tends to obsess on food as it affects physical appearance; calories, fat grams, body weight, dieting. What about the quality of the food? Is it grown with pesticides and herbicides? Is it grown with love, prepared with care, eaten with appreciation? More and more people are choosing to buy organically grown (no pesticides, herbicides or reagent fertilizer) foods. Many people are focusing on how they prepare food as well as what ingredients they use. Beauty in presentation has long been an art form.

It's important to learn about nutrition in order to make healthy choices. Nature provides all we need. I have a vegetable garden each summer. I garden organically, using no chemical pesticides or fertilizers, and the vegetables are delicious and plentiful. Not everyone can have a garden, but there are sources of organic produce in nearly every city and town.

We have *emotional imprints* with food. Food plays many roles in our lives, as nourishment and as part of the social structure in families, between friends and in business.

Do you have a particular comfort food? Is there something you want when you are feeling blue? How did it come to be your comfort food? Who first gave it to you? What were the special foods served when you were a child? There may be foods you particularly dislike for emotional reasons as well. What are they? I like real food; fruits, vegetables, grains. I also love sugar, chocolate in particular. It's tricky sometimes to balance out the healthy food and the unhealthy stuff. I strive for balance.

I cook one or two meals each day. I know that many people rarely cook for themselves. I don't think that's healthy. Frozen foods are convenient but they don't compare with fresh. Take-out food is usually high in fat, and you never really know what's in it. Mass produced food is prepared without love for the individual who will eat it.

When I am online and it's time to eat I cook, and I usually eat meals away from my computer. I take time to focus on the cooking and eating. I find that I enjoy my food more, and if there is another person at home with me then I prefer to eat with them rather than in front of the computer, separate from my family member or friend.

Food Awareness

Remember the last thing you ate. Why did you eat it? Were you satisfying physical or emotional hunger or both?

What was the last meal you had. Were the ingredients healthy? Who made it? What presence of mind and heart went into the preparation?

Have you ever had a meal which was prepared with great love? How was it different from meals which weren't?

Have you ever prepared a meal with love? Have you ever lovingly prepared a meal for yourself?

How was food prepared in your home as a child? How does that compare to the way food is part of your life now?

What are the *emotional imprints* you have in connection with food? Is there any way you want to change your relationship with food?

***

Food involves your body, self love and personal expression. The concept of nurturing one's self with food is growing in our culture. Making a meal for a loved one is emphasized, but when we see a person portrayed in the media eating alone they are lonely and rejected. That perpetuates the myth that a person must be partnered to be whole. This relates to Internet use because if you are lonely and isolated you can log on to your computer and make contact with people in cyberspace. If this use of cyberspace is done with awareness of your deepest needs then it can be healthy. If you are using the Internet to escape your lonliness, that won't work. Providing yourself with food which is good for you, tastes good, and is eaten with pleasure can be part of self-love and nurturing; part of fostering awareness of your deep self and wise use of the Internet.

Food as a gift is a powerful gesture. Cooking is creative, and sharing food is a way to create closeness. It's a wonderful gift for a friend, a mate, a child. Food is a traditional gift after funerals and births.

I like to peruse cookbooks for ideas, but I rarely use recipes. Cooking, for me, is intuitive. It's fun to make something for someone, and for myself.

Take time to prepare a meal; something new or something you've had and enjoyed. The more pleasure you experience cooking, the more pleasure you'll receive in the eating. Food prepared with love is more nourishing than food from an assembly line because it nourishes more than just the body. Remember that thoughts and feelings are quantum events. The intentions and feelings we put into the food affect the person who eats the food.

Love & Food

Think of someone you love. Imagine preparing a meal for them which will be nourishing and which they will enjoy. Visualize the whole thing, including serving them with love, their response and how you feel. Have you ever done this? Would you like to? Is there anyone in your life you would like to offer this to? Has anyone ever done this for you? How would it feel to give or receive such a gift?

What do you put into your body? How do you take it in? Is it a loving gift you give yourself? Think of the food you have eaten in the last week.

These questions are meant to increase awareness, not to judge. Food is so personal that I hesitate to put my strong opinions here, but I have done so, hoping that you will consider my words and not be offended if we are not in agreement.

I don't eat other mammals, birds, fish, crustaceans for many reasons. One is health. The higher up on the food chain one eats, the more complex the organism ingested, the more toxins there are in the food. Toxic chemicals like pesticides, herbicides, radioactive dust from nuclear accidents, are concentrated in flesh and fat. This is because the organism has ingested these substances in their food and stored them in their flesh and fat. Each creature that eats another creature receives a more concentrated dose of toxins. That is not healthy for my body. I also believe that cancer is more likely to occur in people who eat flesh. Since cancer is proteinous cell division gone amok, I believe that supplying the body with excess protein can contribute to cancer. I have proven to myself, being a vegetarian for the last 12 years, that there is plenty of protein available to me without eating meat.

Meat production is an inefficient way to produce food. It takes 10 pounds of grain to produce each pound of meat[9]. That 10 pounds of grain can feed ten times as many people as 1 pound of meat.

I also have moral and spiritual beliefs about eating flesh. The raising of fellow creatures for slaughter is a holocaust. I think of the feed lots for cattle being raised for slaughter, and the chicken factories, and I think of Auschwitz. The Nazis determined exactly what they could get out of the bodies of their victims; hair to stuff pillows with, fat for soap, ashes for cement, etc. Modern consumption of animals is the same; flesh for food, skins for leather, hooves for glue etc. I imagine coming from another world and seeing how some creatures of this world enslave others, keeping them in pens so they can kill and eat them. It looks barbaric and cruel to me.

The animals die in fear, smelling death. The chemicals of fear are in their meat. People eat the meat, ingesting the terror of dying cattle. How can that possibly be healthy?

I tell you these things because they are powerful to me, and I want to offer them to you. Sharing deeply held beliefs is part of creating community. The Internet is the greatest community building medium in history. What you and I do, online and off, impacts all of humankind.

Whatever you believe, it's important that you respect your own beliefs, not that you agree with mine. I encourage you to view food as a source of more than just physical nourishment but as part of the whole context of self love. Caring for yourself is a contribution to the global community.

14.
Solitude and Contact

I crave solitude. I find it relaxing, nourishing, creative, peaceful. Sometimes it's just about having time to do what needs to be done. When I am online I have my solitude and a form of contact with people. The best of both worlds! Solitude can also be a trap leading to isolation and cyber-addiction. If you need time to yourself it's important to get it in ways that allow you deep inner contact, not just distraction. Time alone isn't just about not being with others, it's also about really **being** with your self.

I need time with my friends. Being with people I love, who love me, nourishes me. Whether we are talking, listening to music, walking quietly in the woods, engaged in a task or just hanging out, the contact adds a wonderful sense of belonging to my life.

We all need time alone and time with people. It's important to recognize what those times are. Our childhood experiences figure largely into how we see our needs for contact and solitude.

Growing up in our house it was usually quiet. If people were home there was rarely activity. Cleaning was the exception. My mother went on cleaning frenzies.

I spent much of my time in my bedroom playing fantasy games with stuffed animals and Legos. As a family we were separate most of the time. We came together for meals or the rare family event, like traveling to see our grandparents in New York City. These were tense times due largely to my parents badly strained relationship. The most comfortable place for me was by myself.

I am the youngest of 4 brothers. We were not close as kids. When I was little I used to get up early in the morning and hang out in the kitchen with my oldest brother, Adam. He's 10 years older than I am, and we had fun. I remember meeting him in the kitchen early before sunrise, and his telling me "Sloppy Joe's ain't open yet" and then fixing me a snack. My brother Erich is 5 years older than I, and wasn't any fun. I don't think he and I ever played together. He was sullen, and in retrospect I see how unhappy he was. Jonathan, 3 years older, lived in a room on the ground floor which doubled as the family library. I remember going into his room early on Sunday mornings and playing. He scared me by pretending he was dead. I fell for it every time. Spending time with my Mother was usually sad because she was so depressed. I would have done anything to make her feel better, but nothing worked. I didn't spend much time with my father. When I did it involved his instructing me in Chess or reading classical literature.

In my family I learned to find comfort in solitude, and to be wary of contact with others. As I have grown older I've grappled with how to balance my need for solitude with my need for safe, nurturing contact with others.

The Internet can provide a kind of pseudo-intimacy. It cannot replace being with people in the flesh. For anyone who has **emotional imprints** about connecting with others, which is most of us, it is important to be aware of when time online is serving as a substitute for time with people, and to question this.

Contact Awareness

Remember the house you grew up in. If you lived in more than one then focus on the one which first comes to mind. Was there much activity? What kinds of sounds were there? Did people talk with each other? How did people relate to each other? Were you encouraged to be with people or to be alone or both? Did people talk about their feelings? Were some feelings OK to talk about and not others?

Find yourself in a crowd; a marketplace, a theater, somewhere populated. How do you feel? What do you notice about your response to being around many people? Notice your thoughts, emotions, physical responses. Practice **grounding**. Does your experience change in any way?

Be alone. Notice how you respond to being by yourself. Notice your thoughts, feelings, body. Practice **grounding**. Does your experience change?

Spend some time on the Internet. While doing this, be aware of the kind of contact you are having with the people in your physical environment, and the people you are interacting with online (if any.) How is your sense of connection with the people?

Notice your body and emotions in each of these three experiences.

Love   Joy   Anger   Sadness   Fear

What did you discover about yourself from the exercises?

How does your present life accommodate your need for solitude and contact?

Does the way you feel about yourself change when you are alone or when you are with people?

Are you aware of any *emotional imprints* regarding solitude and contact?

***

Many people need solitude for creativity to flow. When I am involved in a creative project I have a tendency to separate time on the project from time with people. Solitude is less distracting and I can focus better. That's where I discover material for writing and painting. Many musicians find that playing with others in "jam sessions" offers juicy environments for exploring. Everyone is different. Take time to experiment.

Solitude Awareness

This exercise is simply about being with yourself alone. Set aside time. Shorter is OK but longer is better. Find a place where you will not be disturbed. Pay attention to the degrees of comfort and discomfort you feel. Notice your thoughts, feelings, and physical sensations.

For part of the time do nothing. Focus on your breath as

if you were meditating, and just be there. Notice the activity in your mind, your observations of your surroundings, but bring your awareness back to yourself.

For part of the time engage in something physical like walking, dancing, stretching.

For part of the time engage in mental activity. Think.

For part of the time focus on feelings. What do you feel?

Love   **Joy**   **Anger**   **Sadness**   **Fear**

Did you benefit from taking the time alone? Have you done this before? Would you do it again? Why? Why not?

Is your sense of your body different when you are alone from when you are with people?

Did you notice any ***emotional imprints*** when you were alone?

***

Identify your needs for time with people, your needs for time alone, and your needs/desires for time online. What do these things offer you?

Solitude and Contact / 118

15.
Creativity

What does the word "creativity" conjure up for you? Do you think of yourself as a creative person? Are there any "I can't" or "I'm not good enough" messages connected to your creativity? Any **emotional imprints**?

Do you spend time online when you'd like to be painting or writing or otherwise expressing your creativity? It's easy to "hang out" online rather than focus on creative expression. The problem with that is you pay a price for it. Your time disappears. Are you avoiding what you might discover if you express yourself?

We are creative beings. It's not an idea, or a potential, but a fact. You are creating right now! You are creating breath moving in and out of your lungs, thoughts in your mind, feelings, perceptions. You are creating new cells in your body. Every person who reads this book will create a different experience. You are the creator of your life now. When you acknowledge that you are the creator of your life in this moment, you are faced with the challenge and opportunity of creating what you want. You are presented with situations and circumstances. What you do with them is up to you.

Awareness of Creativity

Remember what you did yesterday. See yourself in your mind's eye. Was there anything you did that has a style to it which is particularly you? Where did you develop that flair? That flair is your unique self expression, your creativity.

Look around the room you sleep in. What does this room say about who you are? If a stranger were to look at your room, what would they learn about you?

What mark do you want to leave on this world by the time you die? How does who you are add to the flavor of where you work? Your peer group? Your family? What do you contribute that is uniquely *you*?

When you were a child how was your creativity received? Who did you show it to?

Are there creative projects you are involved with? Are there creative projects you think of doing but never do? What do you tell yourself about these projects?

How are you feeling?

Love   **Joy**   **Anger**   **Sadness**   **Fear**

Are you satisfied with the space and time for creative expression in your life? Do you need to change this?

Have you ever shared creative space with others; a small group drawing party for example?

What creative projects are you interested in doing? Do you give yourself permission to do them? What would it take for you to initiate a creative project?

Are you breathing fully? How does your body feel now?

***

If you've been doing the exercises in this book you've been experiencing yourself. You've been learning about your own nature and your connections with others. If you have any desire to express yourself, do it! Whether you want to write, draw, paint, hum or dance, everything which comes from you is creative, is your spirit, universe-moving. Remember that thoughts and feelings are quantum events, and your relationship with the universe is a manifestation of the momentum we discussed earlier.

Most of us have *emotional imprints* about our creativity. Society sets standards about artistic expression. Some art is "good" and some is "bad." Do you believe that? Did anyone ever tell you that you were talented? Did anyone ever tell you that you were not? Did anyone communicate approval or disapproval to you about your creativity? These messages have a huge effect on us as we're growing up. Many people decide that they can't be artistic or creative because of something they were told as a child, and that **emotional imprint** affects them for the rest of their life, keeping them from exploring their creativity.

I always wanted to be a painter. I love color, texture, the making of marks. I told myself "I am no Van Gogh" and "Adam (my oldest brother) is the talented painter in the family."

I inherited a bunch of pens and water-color inks when I was in my early 20's. I spent weekends drawing and painting; playing loud music, lots of food, alone. A few years later a friend gave me some oil paints. It took me years to get the nerve to buy a canvas and some brushes. I felt inhibited about trying these "serious" paints, but when I did I fell madly in love. What an amazing experience! Texture, color; completely different from watercolor inks.

I've made 4 oil paintings. I still have the thought in my head that "I am not really a painter because I don't do it often enough" but when I do paint it is very satisfying, and I learn so much each time I pick up a brush.

You are an Artist

Is there a form of artistic expression you want to try but haven't yet? Consider this list and add to it.

Visual: painting drawing, collage, sculpture, carpentry
Music: singing, playing an instrument
Movement: dance
Writing: poetry, story, essay

In each of these forms there is room for innovation, for discovery. There is room for you!

Focus on one thing from the list (or from your own list) and say out loud to yourself what it is that you want to do.

"I want to [*fill in the blank*]." Name what it is that you want to do. Naming things is a powerful act. It is a way of making space in your reality for what you are invoking. It is a way of shaping part of the universe to your will.

Say it again. Notice how you feel as you say the words. Say it again only this time louder. And again even LOUDER. Put your passion into it! If this is scary, do it anyway. There is no danger in naming what you want except the danger of change, and change is inevitable.

What would it take for you to do it? Make a plan. What do you need for materials? Space? Time? Identify these needs. Notice any resistance, name it, and proceed anyway. The only thing between you and creatively expressing yourself is an **emotional imprint**. Are you going to allow yourself freedom of expression, or are you going to let the past (or the computer) rule you?

How are you feeling right now? Name it to yourself. That is a creative act of power.

Love   **Joy**   **Anger**   **Sadness**   **Fear**

***

It's easy to spend time online not exploring your creativity. The Internet does offer outlets for creativity but it's not the same as creating something offline. In the digitized cyber world your creativity must fit into the constraints of the medium. This is true with any artistic medium but in the "real world" there is a fluidity not found online.

The fear of creativity is similar to the fear of sex. They are both powerful forces that come from within. They can take you places you've never been. Go to places which defy the constriction of your *emotional imprints*. Remember to ground yourself and allow the fear to pass through you, and go for it!

16.
Home

We need to know that we belong. Much of life is the search for home, whether a physical home, a relationship, or a spiritual home.

Is it possible to feel at home anywhere? Everywhere?

One of the things that the Internet offers to the consistent user is a sense of place. It's odd because cyberspace isn't a physical place, but there are those who find comfort there. This again refers back to the ability to be in control, as much as the medium allows, and more importantly to focus on the imaginal. A chat room is, for the regulars there, whatever they want it to be, no matter what there physical life is like. The sense of familiarity, whether with a chat environment or with surfing the web, offers comfort.

When our umbilical cord was cut we were disconnected from our first home, mother's womb. That created an **emotional imprint**. How it affects us is different from person to person. Some births are smooth transitions, while some are traumatic. Each person is **imprinted** by their unique birth experience.

We are guests on this planet, in these houses, in our bodies. Conversely, it is also true that everywhere is home, mine and yours. I am at home everywhere because my presence is temporary everywhere I go. The universe is my home.

Awareness of Home

Remember when you felt at home and comfortable. Remember the people who were there. Remember the physical place and your own emotional state. What was it that allowed you to feel comfortable?

If you've never felt at home imagine what it might be like. What would you want it to be like?

Remember a time when you felt out-of-place, uncomfortable. Remember the place, the people, your state of mind. What was it that created those feelings?

In thinking about these things notice your different responses. Here is an opportunity to observe *emotional imprints* concerning "home,"a pretty powerful place.

Do you feel at home anywhere in your present life? Where? What is creating that? Do you feel at home in your body?

If you breathe fully, and relax, does your sense of "home" change in this moment? If you are uncomfortable somewhere and you focus on your awareness, can you alter your discomfort?

Is there anything that you have experienced which gives you a sense of belonging?

Can you recreate a sense of being "at home" in a variety of circumstances? Have you tried? What would that entail for you?

***

Do you feel "at home" where you live? How at home are you in cyberspace? What are the differences and similarities in your answers? Does that tell you anything about what's going on in your life?

Allow yourself a sense of "home" wherever and whenever you can, and see how it affects your life.

17.
Suffering

There is suffering every day in our world. It exists in many forms; physical, emotional, spiritual. Each of us experiences suffering in our lives. We suffer because we desire something other than what we have.

The Four Noble Truths of Buddhism:

"Life contains suffering. All existence is in a state of impermanence and unreality."

During our lives we will feel pain, we will suffer. Everything is in a state of constant change, including our suffering. Our personal sense of reality does not define objective reality.

"The cause of suffering is ignorant craving."

Suffering is caused by desire for what we do not have. Anything other than acceptance of this moment creates suffering.

"The suppression of suffering can be achieved."
Suffering cannot be avoided, but we don't have to let it run our lives.

"The way out of constant suffering is the noble eightfold path."

The Noble Eightfold Path

Right Thought
Right Resolution
Right Speech
Right Behavior
Right Means of Livelihood
Right Effort
Right Mindfulness
Right Meditation

The word "right" is not meant to engage you in a conflict about right and wrong, but to suggest that you trust what you feel is congruent with your deepest self. You have a sense of what really "fits" and what doesn't. Be guided by your connection with the universal.

If we fully accept what is happening now then we are in that experience and do not wish for something else. It isn't wrong to desire, it is part of human nature. It does, however, lead to suffering. Since everything is changing, including our suffering, there is no use in suffering over our suffering. It will pass.

It is possible to live with awareness of your suffering, learning from it but not controlled by it. Knowing that it will pass, allowing yourself to feel and go through it, will keep you from getting stuck in it. There are no guarantees.

Develop your consciousness, your awareness, your intentions in relation to how you live. Get to know your ways of thinking, your commitments, your communication patterns. Let your actions come from awareness rather than from automatic responses: your feeding/housing/clothing yourself, your work in the world, your relationships with others. Focus on your existence as a part of the universe. These essential aspects of being human may seem like a tall order but you have your whole life to work on them. We all do.

People ask "Why did this thing happen?" "What did I do to deserve this?" "Is there something bad about me?" "Did I do something wrong?" "Am I not good enough to deserve happiness?" "Am I lovable?" "How can I manage this?" It boils down to "Am I good enough?" We have all pondered these questions in some form at one time or another.

We seek answers through religion, politics, relationships, art, etc. This has been going on for as long as we have been sentient. Different belief systems offer different answers. Redemption through acceptance of a savior or holy martyr, through the belief in karma and a cyclical pattern of spiritual evolution over many lifetimes. Many people embrace the idea of a universal life force. Many accept that there are no definitive answers. For some the answers lie in providing service to others. Some are committed to political solutions, some to artistic ones. What we have in common is we all suffer, we all ask "Why?" and we all find ways to cope with not knowing. Some methods of coping are healthier than others but ultimately each individual makes her/his own choice throughout life, and lives with the consequences.

I hope you've tried some or all of the exercises in this book. They give you tools for staying healthy and exploring spirituality and not losing yourself in cyberspace. Your willingness to do the activities has given you deeper awareness of your connection to the life force and the universe. That awareness can be a rich ongoing part of your life if you wish it.

Life is about awareness, change, and learning. We all make our own meaning. There will be painful moments and joyful ones. You can't hide from life in cyberspace, but you can enrich your life through wise use of cyberspace.

What is important to you? Love? Sex? Spirituality? Materialism? Ecology? There are many questions which we can't answer. We can be aware, though, and revel in the conscious experience of being alive even when we do not have answers. In meditation my focus is to notice the mind and to witness it, not to identify with its activity. I do not need to identify with my questioning, but simply be aware of it.

Asking questions allows you to deepen your awareness. Being identified with your questions, or invested in finding definitive answers, can lead you to become stuck in the past and to miss out on the present. But we do question and we do carry the past within us. Is that another paradox?

Epilogue

I wrote this book because I wanted to share. This material is at once simple and complex, and extends far beyond the Internet in scope and impact.

I hope that you take seriously what you've done while using this book; your ability to create your life using the information and exercises. I hope you feel both challenged and supported by the awareness activities.

The more we each take responsibility for our own awareness, the more we contribute and receive.

Many people have children; an awesome responsibility. Children need to be brought up with good food, opportunities to be creative and inquisitive, and time with nature. Children raised this way will be healthier, more readily aware, than children who aren't. Children are the future of our species.

Children nowadays are practically weaned on computers. If we want them to be healthy contributors to the world it makes sense to teach them to use online media with consciousness. We model this by developing consciousness ourselves.

The Internet is dynamic, constantly evolving as its users shape it. It can be a powerful force for growth and awareness if we make it so.

You have initiated your own inner exploration by reading this book. Let your sense of discovery grow and take you deeper. You have so much to share.

Appendix - Resources

Books:

InGathering by Zenna Henderson

'Till We Have Faces
The Chronicles of Narnia
The Great Divorce
Out Of The Silent Planet
Perelandra
That Hideous Strength all by C.S. Lewis

Dreaming The Dark
The Spiral Dance
Truth Or Dare
The Fifth Sacred Thing
Walking to Mercury all by Starhawk

The Mists Of Avalon
The Darkover Series by Marion Zimmer Bradley

The Lenses Of Gender by Sandra Lipsitz Bem

The Book Of Lilith by Barbara Black Koltuv, Ph.D.
Inanna Queen Of Heaven And Earth by Diane Wolkenstein and Samuel Noah Kramer

The Hidden Life Of Dogs by Elizabeth Marshall Thomas

Survival Into The 21st Century by Viktoras Kulvinskas

A Brief History of Time by Stephen Hawking

Alice in Wonderland
Through the Looking Glass by Lewis Carrol

Illusions by Richard Bach

The Artists Way by Julia Cameron

Peace Pilgrim: Her Life and Work in her Own Words
compiled by some of her friends

Film:

Why Is The Bodhi-Dharma Leaving For The East?

The Lion In Winter

Harold And Maude

Wings of Desire

Notes

Chapter 2

pg. 14
1.   "...if the universe is really completely self-contained, having no boundary or edge, it would have neither beginning nor end: it would simply be." pg. 141 <u>A Brief History of Time</u> by Steven Hawking, Bantam Books 1988

pg. 15
2. pg. 658 <u>Oxford American Dictionary</u> Oxford University Press, Inc., 1980

Chapter 3

pg. 18
3. Having to do with quantum theory, a theory of physics based on the assumption that energy exists in indivisible units.

Chapter 3

pg. 19
4. The word "remembering" can be taken literally to mean re-membering, putting back together.

Chapter 4

pg. 35
5. "Immanent value cannot be rated or compared. No one, nothing, can have more of it than another. Nor can we lose it. For we are, ourselves, the living body of the sacred." "Immanent value does not mean that everyone is innately

good, or that nothing should ever be destroyed. What is valued is the whole pattern, which always includes death as well as birth." pg. 15 <u>Truth or Dare</u> by Starhawk, HarperCollins, 1990

Chapter 5

pg. 39
6. The newspaper article was about a man who beheaded his 14 year old son as the boy was trying to protect his younger brother. The father had been attempting to behead the younger boy. The older boys head was found on the highway where the father had thrown it out of his car as he drove away from the scene.

Chapter 10

pg.78
7. I am not referring to Multiple Personality Disorder.

pg. 86
8. <u>The Sexual Brain</u> by Simon Levay, MIT Pr, 1993
<u>The Science of Desire: The Search for the Gay Gene and the Biology of Behavior</u> by Peter Copeland and Dean Hamer, Touchstone, 1996
<u>The Search for the Biological Origins of Sexual Orientation</u> Rick Kot and Chandler Burr, eds., Hyperion, 1996

Chapter 13

pg. 111
9. <u>Diet For A Small Planet</u> by Frances Moore Lappe, Ballantine, 1992

Illustrations